W9-DFL-266

CANARIES
ON THE RIM

THE HAYMARKET SERIES

Editors: Mike Davis and Michael Sprinkler

The Haymarket Series offers original studies in politics, history and culture with a focus on North America. Representing views across the American left on a wide range of subjects, the series will be of interest to socialists both in the USA and throughout the world. A century after the first May Day, the American left remains in the shadow of those martyrs whom the Haymarket Series honors and commemorates. These studies testify to the living legacy of political activism and commitment for which they gave their lives.

CANARIES
ON THE RIM

Living Downwind
in the West

◆

CHIP WARD

VERSO
London • New York

First published by Verso 1999
© Chip Ward 1999
All rights reserved

Verso
UK: 6 Meard Street, London W1V 3HR
US: 180 Varick Street, New York, NY 10014–4606

Verso is the imprint of New Left Books

ISBN 1–85984–750–1

British Library Cataloguing in Publication Data
A catalogue record is available from the British Library

Library of Congress Cataloging-in-Publication Data
A catalog record for this book is available from the Library of Congress

Typeset in Cochin by Helen Skelton, London
Printed and bound in the USA by R.R. Donnelley & Sons Co.

For Linda

CONTENTS

ONE

LANDING UNDER A
SLEEPING RAINBOW

A child of the East, I had never seen a desert. My eyes had been conditioned to see beauty in the pastoral landscapes of Vermont, the rich forest green of the Adirondaks, and the classic alpine vistas of Switzerland. As I approached Capitol Reef across an open horizon of gray and treeless mesas, I was struck by the bare, unfinished, almost ruined qualities of the land. "My God," I thought, "this is the world's largest construction site."

It was hot and I remember how Factory Butte and Caineville Mesa stood out as if they were all that was left of the surface of the planet after it was excavated. As we drove along, flat cracked plains alternated with huge graceful mounds of muted ash, elephantine evidence of ancient volcanic activity. Maybe it was the Moon. I turned to my wife, Linda, and said, "What the Hell was Bill thinking?"

We were on our way to Capitol Reef National Park to visit Linda's brother, Bill Hauze, who had just landed a job as a seasonal ranger in the heart of Utah's vast complex of redrock canyons. It was our first trip "out West." We were headed for

San Francisco to wear flowers in our hair. Although it was 1973 and the sixties had faded fast, we still regarded ourselves as hippies, two kids just-married, childless and eager to explore. We had vagabonded around Europe the year before and the West was next.

Bill had also lived in Europe. After a couple of years in a German medical school, he became disillusioned with the prospect of practicing Western medicine, which he argued was too focused on dispensing pills to manipulate symptoms rather than understanding and addressing causes and contexts. He had become interested in herbs and chakras long before they were fashionable. I remember sitting on a curb in Cologne and sharing an impromptu lunch of bratwurst and sauerkraut with him while he explained the Sun's influence on the pineal gland and the importance of the resulting metatosin in regulating moods. I thought he might be nuts and humored him. It would be another ten years before I heard about seasonal affective disorder on a television news show.

When he returned to America, for the first time in his life he had no plan. It was exhilarating. A friend offered him a ride to Arizona and he took it. He had never been west of the Mississippi. I wanted to give him a going away gift and came across Ed Abbey's *Desert Solitaire* in a bookstore. I read several pages while standing in the isle and it seemed interesting, so I bought it and gave it to Bill. He read it on his way across the country and was so inspired by Abbey's account of his life as a seasonal ranger in Arches National Monument, Utah, that he made a beeline to Saguaro National Monument near Tucson and talked his way into a job as a seasonal ranger. Capitol Reef was a transfer assignment. Over the years, three brothers, a sister, and his parents would follow his lead and land in Colorado and Utah, a small migration inadvertently set in motion by Ed Abbey's pen.

Eventually, desert gave way to sandstone canyons. We began to relax and look up. My worries about the mental condition of my brother-in-law subsided. I liked what I saw. Redrock is an acquired taste even if you enjoy your first bite. A couple of years later as a guest ranch operator, I had the opportunity to observe how first-time visitors respond to Southwest landscapes that differ radically from the Walden Pond paradigm of Easterners. Most were intrigued and fascinated. Maybe their expectations had already been primed by those coffee-table books by photographers who captured the fractured and stained canyon walls as art. Maybe they had seen John Wayne riding across Monument Valley in *She Wore a Yellow Ribbon* or Robert Redford jumping off a slickrock ledge in *Butch Cassidy and the Sundance Kid*. Even so, it took them a while to appreciate fully what was right in front of their eyes.

A canyon wall may seem beautiful on initial viewing but it is only the first act. Canyons capture light and texture over time. The picture shifts from morning to night, with each passing cloud, and from season to season. Rain changes everything and so does snow. Rain creates dramatic and unexpected waterfalls, washes away dust to reveal new tones of color. Snow outlines canyon wall fracture patterns in bright contrast. Rocks also carry aromas that tell you if they are hot, cold, or wet. And they carry sound, absorbed or echoed, so that the voice of each canyon is different from another. Loving a canyon completely requires the time and patience to wait for all her moods and nuances to appear and reveal themselves to all the senses.

Today, I am thankful I had the opportunity in my life to have that time and find that patience.

Capitol Reef's main claim to fame is its colorful geology, especially the multicolored layers of rock along the Scenic Drive. Spires and domes of white Navajo sandstone sit on top of big broken red walls. Layers of chocolate Moenkopi and pastel mounds of violet, lavender, and gray ash follow beneath. The Navajo name for this phenomenon translates as "sleeping rainbow." In the middle of the park, eleven miles by dirt road from the visitor center and the small Park Service community, was a guest ranch owned by Lurt and Alice Knee, also named the Sleeping Rainbow.

Although at the time we first visited Capitol Reef we did not even dream it, the Sleeping Rainbow was to be our home for almost four years. A year later, during a second visit to the park, we met the Knees and ended up staying. They made an offer and we made a snap decision. We started out caretaking so Lurt and Alice could spend winters in Arizona, warming their old bones and sharing time with dear companions. Eventually, we leased the guest ranch from them and opened it up as our own business.

The "ranch" was actually a long motel unit with a spectacu-lar view that perched on the edge of a small mesa at the conflu-ence of three canyons above Pleasant Creek. It included a log lodge, a house trailer, a cabin, and various out buildings. Alice's Arabian horses galloped through green pastures below. Where it temporarily breaks free of its narrow canyon confines above the Sleeping Rainbow, Pleasant Creek makes a small oasis of tall grasses, cottonwoods, and sagebrush. The profusion of petroglyphs, pictographs, pottery shards, arrowheads, and ancient Anasazi granaries that are found in the area testify that the creek has been "pleasant" for a very long while. A hay shed, some stalls, and a tack room clustered under the shade from a huge stand of old cottonwood trees that once sheltered the Ephraim Hanks polygamist ranch.

Southern Utah's first white settlers were sent down by Mormon leader Brigham Young to colonize the area and look for resources. They endured incredible scarcity and hardship in a landscape that could not have been more alien to those the settlers understood from their English and Scandinavian pasts. Mormon polygamists, fleeing harsh federal laws against their newly adopted theology and lifestyle, also fled south where they hoped they could escape prosecution. Scarcity was also the rule for them, since they brought with them the scant resources of refugees. I often thought of those early white explorers and colonists and wondered what we held in common. Linda and I were also poor, starting out, and unfamiliar with this startling landscape that was so unlike our Eastern environment.

The ruins of the Hanks wives' cabins could be faintly traced on the other side of Pleasant Creek from the Sleeping Rainbow Ranch. Up the creek was a room carved into the rock wall of a canyon with a weathered old door frame built around the entrance. Legend had it that ol' Ephraim and his first wife spent their first winter on the land in that rock room. It is said that the wife became desperate and delusional at one point and Ephraim, fearing she would wander away and get lost, kept her in that stone cell by rolling a stout boulder in front of the door when he left each morning.

True or not, the Hanks were long gone by the time Lurt bought the place in the 1950s. Lurt Knee was originally from

Colorado but his dad was killed while working on the Silverton to Durango train and the family wandered to California. Lurt's sister married Harry Goulding, who had a trading post in Monument Valley. Harry got tired of trying to make a living off of the Navajos alone and went to Hollywood where he camped out in John Ford's office until the director agreed to see the tall cowboy who wouldn't go away. Harry had some photos of the unique landscape around his place. As a result, Ford and other directors were soon making movies in Monument Valley and using Goulding's trading post as a staging area. The lesson was not lost on Lurt, who hunted for a place of his own and found it on the border of what was then Capitol Reef Monument. When the monument became a full-fledged national park, Lurt found himself within its boundaries, an ideal situation that gave him the competitive edge over other local tourist accommodations.

Still, despite his scenic location, he struggled to make ends meet. Utah's redrock deserts were still relatively unknown in the fifties. The hordes of German vacationers, American mountain bikers, and camera buffs you can find on any sunny day today had not yet shown up. So, he tried uranium mining briefly but the mine went nowhere and his first wife left him. Not to be deterred, he eventually found Alice, who had old Philadelphia money and an urge to live in the wilderness.

She was a great big-boned woman with a square face and a high-pitched voice that seemed out of place in such a tall and handsome body. When Lurt met her she was acting as a privately sponsored one-woman peace corps to the Navajo nation. When we told Alice that Linda was pregnant she clapped her hands together, grinned widely, and informed us that although we were seventy miles from the nearest hospital we shouldn't worry. She had delivered two Navajo babies with "nothing but a sharp stick." We cringed, took note, and made sure the gas tank of our car was always full.

Winters were idyllic. In the morning there was time to hunt for cougar tracks in the fresh snow before feeding horses, checking for frozen pipes, and chopping wood. In the afternoon, our chores done, we would hike the trails of Capitol Reef with Bill or read under a crisp cobalt-blue sky. By evening, we would begin the ritual of loading the lodge hearth with pinion and juniper logs to burn for warmth and entertainment. There was no television and only a ham radio at the ranch. Sometimes snow or mud would block the lone road from the ranch to the park border and we would be isolated. Such solitude can test a marriage for compatibility and Linda and I became each other's best friends. There was plenty of time to be lovers, too.

Early spring meant it was time to clear and burn brush away from the irrigation ditches that carried creek water to our garden and pastures. Drifts of tumbleweed that the wind had corralled behind the garden fences over the winter had to be removed so vegetables could be planted. Guestrooms had to be cleaned, repairs made, supplies purchased, advertising lined up, and reservations made. The late spring, summer, and fall were filled with long hours entertaining guests, shopping, cooking, cleaning, and pulling weeds in the one-acre garden where we grew enough food to feed ourselves and the daily load of hungry customers. Even when the days were long and dictated by a rigid schedule for cleaning rooms and preparing and then serving meals, we could still squeeze in time to hike up canyon and splash in the creek to cool off. The nights still pulsed with the sudden light of meteors arcing across a crystalline sky.

When our first child was born, we added tending the baby to our list of cares. We could dote on Brian during the winter in our warm cabin, or carry him with us in a tight yellow sling as we climbed the narrow passage up the cliff wall behind the lodge on our daily trip to a stand of old trees we called "the bonsai grove." There we would look out on Mount Ellen in the distance, where a herd of buffalo still roamed free. We would count our blessings and wander home past ancient Anasazi Indian carvings and a nest of peregrine falcons. Hours passed like prayers, quiet and hopeful. We were humbled and awed by the beauty and mystery unfolding around us.

During our years in the wilderness, we learned compelling, fundamental, and ancient lessons that we had missed during our modern education while immersed in the American Way. For the first time in our lives, the connections between our bodies and the water and soil that nourished us appeared short and simple. Back in the city, water was an abstraction. It poured magically from a tap on an underground network of pipes that drained a faraway reservoir I had never seen and probably couldn't locate offhand. To keep it flowing, I merely paid a bill. At the ranch, our drinking and irrigation water gathered on the Aquarius Plateau and tumbled down the face of Boulder Mountain, our view to the east, where it fed the riparian oasis under our window. I was responsible for clearing the irrigation headgate and ditches of flood debris, cleaning the filters on the drinking water cistern under the lodge, and maintaining the pump that pulled it up from a spring beside the creek. When the pump failed, we literally carried our water each day. One winter we had to melt snow for cooking and drinking when a pipe between the spring and lodge froze.

Our water supply was a daily concern and the cycles that replenished it were at hand and sometimes dramatic. In the summer we could watch thunderheads build and burst, then wait for a flash flood to rumble down Pleasant Creek an hour later. Days later, a carpet of fresh growth would fill in the flood path and deer, bees, and birds would seek the tender grass and wildflowers that embroidered the flood's green wake. Over time, then, if we were attentive and patient enough, the stone-loaded percussion of a flash flood would be followed by a chorus of birdsong and bee buzz.

In eastern America where water is everywhere, water's life sustaining role is hidden in the lush background. In the baked desert lands of the West, water's gift becomes foreground that is underlined boldly. As any desert dweller will readily attest, water is life. Humans, too, are fluid creatures. I do not mean that we are graceful and agile, though some are, but that we blister, bleed, urinate, salivate, sweat, and cry. Our bodies are a community of fluids. While living on the ranch, the ways water reached our habitat from the sky and how we incorporated it became obvious.

Likewise, years of growing the corn, tomatoes, and melons that attracted and pleased hungry guests taught us that the nutrients our bodily fluids carry arise from soil that was once leaf, limb, stone, root, bone, carcass, carapace, and flower. It was churned, swallowed, and excreted by worms, ants, mites, millipedes, beetles, and bacteria so it could feed the plants we tended in our garden that, in turn, used the generous chemical energy of the Sun to make food available to us and our wilderness pilgrims. Under the Sleeping Rainbow, our continual bodily communion with the whole wide world was a biological fact of life and the walls we had built between the personal and the planetary during a previous education melted away.

We made a good life under the Sleeping Rainbow but it was not the life I expected to lead. I had lived in big stimulating cities like New York, Boston, and Cologne. I thought I would teach or become an anthropologist, hobnob with intellectuals and engage in fascinating conversations. Instead, the canyons and desert spoke to me and I stayed to listen carefully. I found out "what the Hell" Bill was thinking. My life, too, was drawn and turned by the land.

There were times while I was living there that I felt guilty. I thought of myself as someone who was involved in the world of politics and committed to causes. During my previous existence, I had marched, sat in, written letters, and gone door to door. In Capitol Reef, I was as socially isolated as I could imagine one could be in this day and age. I had left a familiar and noisy world far behind. Friends from college wrote and worried about me. "You've dropped off the map," they said. "Come back."

Now I know I needed that time and place. The most important lessons of my life were learned there, under the Sleeping Rainbow. Those lessons became the lens for the next phase in my life as we moved to northern Utah and lived on the rim of another desert, the Great Basin, where we raised our kids and made our modest careers. We inadvertently moved from the grandest wilderness area in the contiguous United States to the most extensive environmental sacrifice zone in the nation. In an odd twist of fate, lessons learned living in the wilderness gave me the insight and resolve I needed when I found myself on the rim of apocalyptic ecocide.

The stark contrast of those experiences revealed to me how our bodies are grounded in ecosystems and how we all live downwind and downstream from one another. Those lessons made me understand how the collective decisions we make about what we allow into our air, water, and soil are translated into flesh and blood and living daily experience. I also learned how the mythic West of our pop culture hides a shameful legacy of environmental abuse, toxic wastefulness, and betrayal. This is the story of how I learned those lessons and how I learned to fight back. It is about deserts and how we use them. It is about the people who live on the desert rim, whose unacknowledged suffering should signal a loud warning to us all.

TWO

THE COW THAT GOT STUCK
IN THE CHIMNEY

There was no other creature in the desert as flatulent as the Chimney Canyon ungulate. It was stuck in lower Chimney Canyon and we wanted it out. It crapped in the springs, stripped the canyon floor of much-needed seedlings, cut the stream banks with its hooves so they eroded, and drew thousands of flies to its stinking waste. No native animal in a desert canyon can load a shady redrock alcove with so many layers of fly swarming dung.

Cow shit is the unmistakable, obvious, and defining sign that cows are in an area. There is no animal, bird, or reptile in the arid canyon lands of the West that compares with a cow in this regard. Think about it. When was the last time you walked down a slickrock canyon and exclaimed "PU! That damned lizard shit sure stinks!"? Or, have you ever stepped in a pile of rattlesnake crap so deep you wondered if there was a bottom? Compared with a cow plop, deer turds are a gentle and dignified affair and cougar crap is crude but interesting ("hmm, is that a bit of fur and bone I see?"). A cow can easily poop thirty pounds of pie a day.

Cattle ranchers will tell you cows have a beneficial fertilizing effect on the desert soil, I suppose in the same way that cookie dough on a tin baking sheet has a fertilizing effect on its surface. Cow pies bake and harden so that you can burn 'em or build with them. Until cows are outfitted with little plows to drag behind them wherever they go to mix the foul stuff into the ground, I won't buy that argument. No, considering what happens at the back end of cows, it is clear they are a square peg in the desert's round hole. No niche, no dice.

What happens at the back end, of course, is just half the story. A cow requires a lot of water under the best of circumstances and being stranded in the desert isn't the best of circumstances. Cows are like water-seeking missiles. The front end follows the flow and strips the green that grows beside it, while the legs between the front and back cut and crush it. A single cow can turn a clean spring teeming with delicate diversity into a muddy barren wallow. When you consider that most desert wildlife also rely on fragile "riparian" areas for survival, cows are like the wilderness roommates from Hell. They crap in everyone's drinking water.

In the arid uplands of the desert, where precipitation is scant and crucial to health and renewal, cow impact is just as damaging. Cows kick up dust, compact soils, break down delicate cryptobiotic surfaces that fix nitrogen in the soil, erode hillsides, and chew stressed-out plants down to the nubs. Only the most hardy plant species can survive them, which is why prickly pear cactuses spread in their shit-encrusted wake. Desert animals fare no better. Cow herds can crush out whole prairie dog towns and destroy the homes of other creatures that burrow, a behavior common in the desert. In the San Rafael

Swell, there are some five hundred species of bees that nest in the ground. Smart match, right? Cows and bees.

It would be difficult to design an animal so inappropriately suited for life in a desert as the American breed of cow. A cow doesn't obtain and use its food and water as efficiently as a toad or lizard, though it sure will come out on top if it steps on one. It doesn't have the stealth of a wildcat or the resourcefulness of a rodent. It can't burrow to escape the heat like a fox. It can't climb in and out of canyons like a bighorn sheep or even follow the narrow paths of agile deer that criss-cross the talus slopes. Cows are basically milk and meat machines that we have parked in our food chain for so long that they look perfectly at home in feedlots.

Raising a cow in the desert makes as much sense as growing oranges in Alaska. Of course, the federal government is not building greenhouses for Alaskan orange growers at public expense and then subsidizing their operations annually. We do give that kind of support to desert cattlemen. Even so, a cow in the desert Southwest is just a wrench in the ecological gears, predator bait at best.

Anyone who doubted how mistaken the cow was in the lower end of Chimney Canyon had only to climb into the upper reaches of the canyon where the cow could not go to prove the point. The difference between the cow and non-cow sections of Chimney was dramatic. The cowless upper canyons are lush with a wide range of grasses, trees, and shrubs. Bees buzz and humming birds dart among a riot of wildflowers. The springs there flow clear and the potholes are pristine and lively with delicate insects, frogs, and slim green reeds. Creeks run deep and narrow through lush sheltering banks. Canyon floors are gracefully wooded with cottonwoods, young and old, with firm roots to hold precious soil in place. Birds, deer, mice, and snakes abound where shade and sunlight dance. Once I had seen the diverse and healthy upper reaches of the canyon, I knew the cow had to go. But how?

The cow in Chimney Canyon was stuck. On one end it was cliffed out. On the other was a dry, vast, and forbidding desert. So it stayed, the sole survivor of several cows who were left behind when a lazy rancher failed to remove his entire herd from a grazing allotment in that portion of the San Rafael Swell. The poor bovine refugee belonged in a pasture in Wisconsin or Switzerland where cows with clanking bells waddle about in rich knee-high green. But fate has a twisted sense of humor and stranded it alone in the beige dust and pastel tones of sage in that isolated canyon.

I first encountered the cow on a week-long backpacking trip into the San Rafael Swell, a vast network of slots and broad-shouldered canyons in Utah's colorful redrock region. The San Rafael is a huge slab of the earth tilted up at a crazy angle. Washed by sudden storms and floods over the ages, the San Rafael has eroded into graceful, sometimes weird, patterns in descending scale, so that the same layered shapes you see at your feet are also written large when you look up and scan the horizon. The open sky invites light to play all day on those textured echoes of stone. It is a place of solitude and naked beauty.

We'd saved Chimney Canyon for last because it is so awesome. Chimney is an incredibly unimaginative name for what is actually a network of canyons with amazing painted and sculpted walls. Along with the usual canyon wall paintings that are created when wind and water meet dark redrock varnish, minerals leaching out through the sandstone walls have also made strange pale batik patterns. In some places the white mineral traces look like Arabic script, as if an ancient giant had written a sacred text for the sky to read. One wall is snow white. Others look tie-dyed.

Above the painted panels, minerals had dissolved out of the stone face to form elaborate, intriguing, and bizarre holes. They are scooped and sculpted, pitted and arched, reminiscent of coral reefs or the fanciful spires of the Spanish architect Gaudi. Chimney Canyon is such a plain name for such a spectacular and unique place. It should have been named "gallery canyon," since each turn revealed another breathtaking panel of natural art.

But it could also be called "gut cramp canyon." The same powerful loads of minerals that leached out and decorated the walls with mysterious designs and dissolved to create bizarre sculpturing also seeped into the canyon's drinking water. Sulfur Creek was aptly named. Even the spring we relied on to replenish our water supply was full of bowel-freeing magnesium chloride. If you go there, you have to stay overnight and you have to drink. Diarrhea is the inevitable price of admission to Chimney Canyon. So all things considered, it could have had a worse name, too. The Anglo settlers struggled in this last corner of North America to be explored and settled and their adversarial relationship with the land echoes in the names they left behind. The map of Southwest wilderness is covered with names like Hell's Backbone and Box Death Hollow, Brimstone this and the Devil's that.

Our guide was Steve Allen, who is becoming legendary for his thorough exploration and passionate defense of the canyons of the Colorado Plateau, places like the San Rafael Swell, the Dirty Devil River, and of the vast Escalante wilderness that is now included in our nation's newest national monument, Grand Staircase Escalante. A tall, lanky, lope-legged man with a perpetual grin, Steve Allen has explored every corner of those vast wildlands and knows them like the bottom of his foot. He wears out several pairs of boots every year while hiking.

An outstanding rock climber, he has braved the broken ledges and sheer walls of canyon country to see into its hidden recesses and learn their secrets. His favorite routes follow the faint traces of ancient cliff dwellers who carved "moqui steps" into tilted rock faces that lead in and out of deep canyons that, at first glance, look impossible to reach. When I first started backpacking with Steve, his route-finding abilities seemed incredibly intuitive to me. Then I realized they were honed the hard way over many years of strenuous hiking and patient exploration.

Swooping down dunes with a yellow headscarf flowing over his shoulders, his loose powder-blue doctor scrubs and white dress shirt flapping in the wind, Steve cuts a dashing and romantic figure, like a sheik. But up close and personal, he is a modest and unassuming man with a keen mind, quick sense of humor, and a generous spirit.

Steve had just told us the history of the feral cow and her ancestors. She was a remnant of another era, not long ago, when grazing was imprinted on every corner of the Western landscape without exception. Even the anemic policies we have today that withdraw some cows from some desert areas didn't apply then. Cowboy culture reigned and cows were pushed into every nook and cranny, including Chimney Canyon. Consequently, there is no wild water source in the desert West, even in the most remote wilderness, that is free from the threat of giardea, a protozoan carried and distributed by cows that has the impact of dysentery on those unfortunate enough to encounter it. Although it rarely rains in canyon country, little moisture is absorbed along the steep slickrock surfaces. Drainage is sudden, redundant, and radical. Summer storms are dramatic affairs with flash floods and waterfalls cascading over cliff walls. Whatever is laid on the ground eventually goes to the low spots where water collects. Backpackers who rely on streams, springs, and potholes to replenish their water supplies use filter pumps and iodine tablets to avoid suffering gastric distress. Long before there were uranium tailings, there were cow trailings, the desert's first toxic shock.

Brought to Arizona by the Spanish in the seventeenth century and then to California in the late eighteenth century, cows have been in the West as long as the white people who owned them. The colonial cows of California were set loose on a Mediterranean-like landscape much different from the one we see today. Then, a 22-million acre inland prairie of bunchgrass, oat grass, beardless wild rye, and perennial forbs was surrounded and broken by oak woodlands, forested slopes, thick marshes, and chaparral. In the 1860s, a cattle boom followed in the wake of the Goldrush, and some three million cows were soon chewing up California's open ranges. Degradation was rapid. Overgrazing was aggravated by drought. Drought was followed by floods. In 1863, 97,000 cows were grazing parched Santa Barbara County. Two years later, only 12,000 remained. Ranges were denuded, native plant species disappeared, and desertification began. Ranchers moved their bovine locusts into the Sierra Nevada and the Great Basin from the west, while settlers, dragging and pushing their cattle along beside their wagons, were converging from the east. The Colorado Plateau and the San Rafael were just a step away.

When we express our outrage at the destruction of the Amazon rainforests, we might remember that this is not the first time a vast ecosystem was destroyed to make money. Although the landscape of California and much of the rest of the West looks "normal" to us today, it is not what it once was. A hundred years ago, sitting astride their horses, the first settlers in the northern Utah valley where I live now could barely see over the tall grasses they found there. In less than a hundred years, their great-grandchildren were living in a dust bowl. The buffalo of the Great Plains did not fly away and we all know what happened to the native people who once hunted them. Still, we deny our history and are reluctant to face and fix the mistakes we made when we tried to impose the wet European paradigm of cows in pastures on a vast and dry western landscape.

Cows were spread out quickly wherever whites settled because there was precious little pasture and competition for grazeable ground was stiff. A cow turned out to graze east of the Mississippi, where the vast majority of cows hang out, requires a handful of acres to chew on and live. In Western deserts, it may take hundreds of acres to provide the same support. After all, a foraging cow can eat several hundred pounds of vegetation a month. Every imaginable patch of grass was eventually found and exploited—and our dogged ranching pioneers had big imaginations. They often saw grass that wasn't there.

Once feed and water were discovered, they would do anything to get their cows to it. Near Capitol Reef, I once followed an old steep and jagged cow path to the top of a spring-fed mesa meadow. The rock faces along the trail were streaked with the long black skid marks cattle hooves made as they gouged their way to the top or slid down the slick rock slopes along the way. I couldn't imagine how you could get cows up and down such steep and treacherous angles until I remembered snarling cowdogs and whips. In the more recent past, bulldozers have blazed trails through the rugged terrain so that cows can just amble until they find water, which is first on their list of what they must do to survive in the alien heat.

By the time the Chimney Canyon cow's stranded and pregnant mother bore her, cattle grazing dominated not only those forested mountains and high valleys where there were meadows and pastures, but also the harsh dry deserts of the American West. Today, about 85 percent of the Bureau of Land Management's mostly arid land is open to grazing, including wilderness and wilderness study areas. Most of our National Forest land and even some national parks are open to cheap below-cost grazing. Yet only 3 percent of the nation's beef supply comes off of public lands. If grazing on public land was ended tomorrow, hardly a blip would appear on McDonald's radar screen, but it would be a sea-change for the health of Western ecosystems and their wildlife. Most of the cattle that would be displaced are owned by big operations that function as tax-sheltering investments for even bigger corporations. Even weekend ranchers who don't make a living raising cattle use their hobby as a means to write-off the costs of the new pick-up trucks they drive. If grazing was ended on public lands, the corporations would move their money elsewhere and weekend ranchers would have to settle for driving last year's model. Life would go on as usual for most citizens of the West.

Don't get me wrong, Steve said. All public land grazing is not harmful and, yes, there are many hard-working, all-American, salt-of-the-earth ranchers who depend on federal land for grazing. Grazing has its place. But the desert is not that place and the Chimney Canyon cow was a case in point. It was hard to listen to Steve and ever see a hamburger the same way again. After one trip with him, I walked into a river-runners tavern and ordered a "root of all evil sandwich."

Critics of grazing, like Steve Allen, argue that the history of grazing in the arid West and the damage cows did there illustrates how unconscious we are of our natural physical environments. Early settlers might be excused for not understanding how mismatched cows and deserts are, but our persistence in putting cattle into deserts today reveals willful ignorance, abstraction, denial, and reckless arrogance that cannot be excused. We can sing "home, home on the range" all we want, but after hundreds of years, we remain strangers on this land. The cow in Chimney Canyon was an artifact of our history of profound disconnection with our desert ecosystems.

At some point, the damage that should have been predictable was so obvious, even to those government stewards who were not inclined to look for it, that minimum land-use criteria were recognized and sometimes enforced. Permission to graze cows in some areas was temporarily withdrawn to let them "rest" and some harsh allotments were simply abandoned.

The rancher who abandoned Chimney Canyon did a poor job of rounding up his cows and herding them away. Several cows managed to avoid capture and a forced march back to the barbed-wired enclosures of rodeoland. They remained all year round to spread their stumble and muck mess. Steve had been pressing the BLM for years to clean up the bad act that was left behind, but to no avail. Nature was faster than the feds. One by one the stray cows died of natural causes while the debate raged on. To add insult to injury, Chimney Canyon was slated for a return to grazing.

The strays died off, but at least one was pregnant and produced a big black and white beast before she lived out her lonely life crapping up and chomping down Chimney Canyon. This only surviving offspring was the last feral remnant of the BLM's botched job. As Steve finished his account, we rounded a bend, and there she stood. She looked up and saw us immediately. Her reaction was a lot like mine would be if I awoke and found a Martian standing over my bed. Her eyes bulged with terror and she spun around and did a wheelie out of there. In her lifetime, she had only encountered a handful of humans and, judging from her response, we were hideous. We chased after her until her dust choked us and she was safely around the bend. I'm not sure what we would have done if we had caught up to and cornered her. We had neglected to bring our snarling dogs and whips. We walked on.

After we saw her, we saw what she had done to the lower part of the canyon. Then we started to plan. When we returned to civilization, we flooded the local BLM office with angry letters. Get the cow out! Now!

It was clear from the beginning the agency was in no hurry and didn't understand the fuss. The contrast between the BLM's attitude towards this bovine alien destroying the lower Chimney Canyon ecosystem and its approach to any wild natural predator that threatens a single cow was particularly outrageous to me. The agents in charge of Western federal lands would have no hesitation in calling up a sharpshooter in a helicopter if a cougar was even suspected of harming some rancher's sheep or cow.

In the war between economy and ecology, economy has been winning. In a typical year, our government pays more than $40 million of our tax dollars to kill approximately 80,000 coyotes, 7,000 foxes, 1,500 bobcats, 9,000 beavers, 4.6 million birds, and 300 bears. In all the hundreds of days I have spent quietly exploring remote canyons, I have never seen a live cougar. But in a typical year, the feds slaughter about 300. That number is small compared with the number legally killed through the issuance of special hunting permits by states that are another means of reducing predators. In 1997, state wildlife agencies in Utah alone allowed hunters to kill 576 mountain lions. The death count attributable to cattlemen and sheepherders acting on their own while the feds and state officials look the other way is not available. We got a glimpse of what might be going on, however, in 1991 when Wyoming's state predator control manager was busted for the illicit sale of enough pilfered strychnine, cyanide, and thallium sulfate to kill every man, child, and predatory mammal in the US.

We are not only driven to eliminate predators because they are perceived as a threat to cattlemen's profits, they are also seen as a threat to state revenues. State fish and game agencies, affectionately referred to by their employees as "the Division of Hooks and Bullets," manage wildlife for those willing to pay license fees to kill it. Deer, for example, are a "harvestable" resource. Cougars just eat the profits. They are being wiped out to protect deer populations that are thinning, not from too many cougars but from habitat loss as housing developments spread through foothills and shopping malls and parking lots replace valley forage.

Why such a wildlife holocaust? There is little evidence that predator control makes much difference. Most cow losses are from disease and weather. In a typical year in Montana, only one-tenth of 1 percent of the calf crop is killed by predators. This is only 2 percent of all cattle losses. If predator killing was stopped tomorrow the loss of cows would go up, but not much. The losses would be greater for sheep that are smaller and more vulnerable than cows, but there are other ways to protect sheep that have been practiced for centuries. If you are one of the few lucky ranchers who benefit from state-funded predator control, however, why buy a sheepdog or llama to guard your herd when the ADA trapper is just a phone call away and he'll do the job for free?

The ADA, or Animal Damage Control, is the little-known federal agency that does most of the sanctioned killing. It was established in 1931 when the federal war on predators was codified. Having slaughtered the Indians and buffalo that were in the way of the settlers and their cattle, we aimed our weapons at those lesser troublesome inhabitants of the Western ecosystems we were determined to manipulate and make pay. The Act establishing the ADA even includes "ground squirrels, rabbits, and other animals injurious to agriculture" in its charge "to conduct campaigns for the destruction and control of such animals." It's a wonder those San Rafael bees weren't included, since the cattle probably find them annoying. ADA's arsenal includes leg traps, strangling snares, cyanide-firing traps hidden in carrion, aerial gunning, and "denning." Denning means gassing or burning coyote pups in their den or dragging them out with hooks and then clubbing them to death.

We even kill when there is clear evidence that killing doesn't work. In fact, killing predators can make matters worse. For example, a natural pack of coyotes, undisturbed in the wild, is socially stable. Older males lead and younger males follow. Coyotes mate for life and female fertility cycles are in sync with habitat carrying limits so that overpopulation does not occur. A group of coyotes has a territory and they know how to exploit its food resources successfully without going after animals like sheep and cows that are not part of the natural food web.

When hunters are paid to go after coyotes, when coyotes are trapped and poisoned by ranchers, and when cattle chase out the prairie dogs and other burrowing game that coyotes eat, the natural dynamic is upset. Killing breaks down the pack's hierarchy so it resembles a gang of leaderless adolescents. When coyote couples are broken up by killing and pups die, the dynamic mating cycles are radically altered, resulting in fierce competition for females. Hormonal storms rage through the pack. As packs are broken up and disbursed or simply pushed away from their territories, coyotes end up competing for food in unfamiliar areas and cannot efficiently exploit their natural food webs. All this turmoil can turn a coyote into a calf killer. The ADA, then, is really in the business of fulfilling its own prophecies about the danger of predators. The agency's mission of ridding the predator-rich ecosystems of the West of predators will always recede before its futile and cruel policies.

Early in our campaign to remove the cow from Chimney Canyon, BLM agents were challenged simply to walk into Chimney Canyon and shoot the animal. After all, it belonged to no one and would not be missed. Given the government's complicity in the slaughter of wildlife and its inclination towards violence, this did not seem like an unreasonable expectation. No way, they replied. Shooting a cow in Utah is not politically possible. The notion of shooting a cow on federal land is so offensive to cattlemen and their elected allies that to order such an act would guarantee a short and miserable career for a BLM agent. Given the militia mood of the rural West, such an act could even be personally dangerous.

There was a brief discussion among the band of outraged letter-writing hikers about how a couple of us could slip into the canyon in the winter when no one was around and do the dirty deed ourselves. However, no one owned a gun or knew how to use one. Except me. I explained to them that I owned a shotgun and we would need a high-powered rifle. Trying to kill a cow with buckshot from far away would be difficult. I'd have to wound it, chase it, wound it, catch up and shoot it again until it finally keeled over. I might be willing to shoot a cow but I wasn't up to conducting the aerobic torture of some dumb beast in the middle of Paradise. The karmic implications were too heavy. I might come back in my next life as a dartboard. The gun option was finally dropped because it was outside the rules. The West has enough vigilantes.

When we got loud enough and it was clear we were not going away, the BLM hired wranglers and sent them out to capture the cow. But the wranglers reported they were unable to get their horses up a shattered portion of the trail leading into the canyon and so they went no farther. A real wrangler doesn't hike, an activity they associate with lowland sissies and one that is also impeded by their preference for skintight denim pants and loose boots with high heels. The remains of a campfire and an empty whiskey bottle that we discovered later told the story. They hadn't tried very hard. When asked what the cow looked like, the cowhands exchanged quick, blank looks and it was clear they never even saw her. They were, as they say, close enough for government work. Our run-amok cow had no reason to fear the feds. If it had been ensconced in Bombay, it couldn't have been better protected.

We renewed our letter writing and phone calling, keeping the pressure on until the BLM offered a deal. If Steve would round up some volunteers to go in and repair the old trail leading into Chimney Canyon so wranglers could get their horses in, the BLM would send the wranglers back in to capture the cow and lead it out. BLM rangers would go in to inspect the trail repair and would also accompany the wranglers to see that the job got done. Once the cow was out, it would be sold at an auction, though probably not for much since it was tough and wiry. We Americans may be oblivious to the cow misery we eat for dinner, but we do notice if it is tender and juicy. In the end, someone would kill the Chimney Canyon cow anyway, maybe to feed to their dogs. It sounded like a lot of work to rescue a cow that would end up taking a dirt nap anyway, but I agreed at once to be part of the crew. Any excuse to hike in the wilderness is a good one.

*

The trail crew was Steve Allen, myself, a young couple from California, and Ginger Harmon. Ginger is one of my role models in life. I hope to be half as active, committed, and vigorous as she is in her mid-sixties when I reach that age. Ginger raised a family and built a business with her husband. Then, when the nest was empty, she split for Nepal where she led hikes into the Himalayas. She next wrote a book on hiking Europe for the Sierra Club and then joined the board of the Southern Utah Wilderness Alliance. There, her wise countenance nurtured staffers and her shrewd and persistent work on behalf of wilderness aggravated would-be despoilers. Ginger spends her winters skiing in Idaho and the rest of the year backpacking in between meetings and political campaigns. She can climb with ropes as well as anyone half her age and has figured out how to go light. She never carries a tent but curls up in small sandstone hollows that those of us who hike with her affectionately call "Ginger holes." And no mattress, too.

Since she left the SUWA board, Ginger has devoted her time and energy to the Great Old Broads for Wilderness, a group of clever middle-aged and older women who, like Ginger, still backpack the Southern Utah wildlands and are determined to defend them against cows, road builders, and petty parochial politicians. They monitor grazing permits for sensitive lands, both in the field and in the BLM's files. They show up at hearings, make phone calls, write letters, lobby, produce a newsletter, and speak out publicly every chance they get. And somehow, they also manage to have lots of fun and outdoor adventures.

The hike into Chimney Canyon was wonderful—a startling deep blue October sky above and crisp rain-scrubbed horizons all around. We arrived near dusk, ate dinner, and turned in. Ginger found a Ginger hole. I slept under a glimmering lattice of stars so bright it woke me up twice to pay amazed attention from my little resting place in the sand. We set to work early the next morning and by afternoon we had moved enough rocks and dirt into place along the old broken stock trail that we called it good and went on to explore an upper canyon. That night, we slept soundly beneath a crystalline sky pulsing with bright stars.

Five BLM rangers met us the next day. The rangers had driven as far as they could and then hiked. They hadn't escaped from their offices often that year and when they had they were usually anchored to their pickup truck seats, so they arrived winded and sweated. Awkward introductions followed and then an inspection of the repaired trail. It was judged satisfactory. Good work, they said, and thank you.

A Steve Allen tour of the cow-free upper Chimney Canyon highlighted the day. He showed them the painted and sculpted walls. We climbed up to a spooks gallery of hollow-eyed and howling sandstone gargoyles carved by wind and water into one canyon wall. We examined a huge packrat midden tucked into a crevice that had probably been inhabited and added to for a thousand years. We followed clear streams through narrow canyons that were over our heads in wild grasses and rare tropical-looking desert plants. One ranger, a "national expert" on grass species, found two kinds he had never seen before. Another ranger announced he had never seen riparian areas as healthy as these.

Myriad birds announced our presence as we entered each side canyon. In one narrow passageway, a deer that we startled hurtled down from above and we had to throw ourselves tight against the canyon wall to keep from being slammed and trampled. We saw a pygmy rattlesnake. As I recounted how often I had seen rattlers there, one of the rangers used the word "infested," a revealing choice since the abundance of snakes was an indication of the area's robust health and plentiful supply of small animals to eat. I bet he never used that word on a cow.

The rangers kept Steve in front busy with questions about the lay of the land they had studied often but didn't know while Ginger gently chided them about their pro-cow policies from behind. Throughout our walk it became clear that these guys who were charged with managing and protecting these wild desert lands for the good of the nation and generations to come had no idea before that afternoon that such hidden splendor existed. They could not have known the true character and beauty of Chimney Canyon from a contour map, aerial photo, resource inventory or any of the other document descriptions they use to do their duty. It all looks like politics and dollar signs if you look from too far away. It doesn't catch the breath or quicken the heart from behind a desk. This was jaw-dropping beautiful and they couldn't hide their blown-away response. That night by the campfire we won our case. They promised they would be back and the cow would be out. Next week.

And so it came to pass. I was notified two weeks later by letter. Thank you for your efforts, they said, the cow is out. Mission accomplished.

But that's not the end of the story. Weeks later I learned that the expedition of rangers and wranglers had reached the canyon as planned, crossed over our rebuilt trail well enough, found and captured the errant cow as hoped, and then the whole scheme went to Hell in a handbasket as we say out West. The cow was terrified. It resisted. The usual methods were applied. Ropes were tightened. Horses pulled. Dogs snapped. Wranglers yelled and slapped. Rangers prodded. After grueling hours of struggling to get the reluctant prisoner back to a loading point along an old mining road where a truck was waiting, the desperate cow lunged at one of its tormenters, slipped, and fell four feet into a ravine. Cowboys followed, lest the wily cow escape, but found her crumpled and unable to stand. She had shattered her leg. In the official report, a BLM staffer wrote that he "dispatched her with a single round from my .45 caliber Sig Sauer duty weapon."

A sad ending: the poor cow was tortured and killed, one more casualty in the great Western land wars. We have warred with each other—white men versus Indians, Anglos versus Mexicans, cattlemen versus sheepherders, and now conservationists versus cattlemen, miners, and lumbermen. We have warred with the land's natural creatures—buffalo, bears, wolves, coyotes, and cougars. We have warred with the land itself—building dams and moving rivers, flooding canyons, strip mining, chaining, burning and abandoning our waste on desert floors. We have created an army to manipulate and manage the land and its "resources" for marginal gains to a handful of powerful stakeholders. And the land has suffered wherever our restless and confused hands have been set upon it. The land we have not reached with our roads, fences, mines, oil and gas wells, pipelines, and cows is still the healthiest and most beautiful. But we have no measure for soul-soothing inspiration and we refuse to calculate the true cost of our addictions to beef, gold, and oil. We have produced a billion words of rules and regulations, schedules and contracts, assessments and studies, to guide our clumsy reach, but the word "sacred" does not appear once. Those that manage do not know.

A happy ending: nature tends to balance, heal, and make whole. Riparian areas are resilient. Within just a few years, the once cow-churned banks of Chimney Canyon Creek are firm and full of tall grasses where deer graze and birds and mice nest. Flowers have returned, too, and the contented murmur of bees fills the air where flies once swarmed. Young cottonwood trees, the first to thrive in decades, are now joining their old forebears along the canyon floors. At night, as stars blaze above and frogs croak and call below, bobcats, foxes, and cougars sip from clear springs and potholes. The BLM rangers who hiked Chimney Canyon with us were so impressed by what they experienced, grazing was not renewed there. Because people who cared persisted. Across the West, there are people like Steve Allen and Ginger Harmon who can see and appreciate desert ecosystems for what they are and respond to the needs they perceive. They have a clear sense of place and are determined to protect the good stuff that is left after so much blind greed and folly. And in another small corner of the American landscape, health has been restored.

A warning: deserts are misunderstood and vulnerable. We are not a desert people. White Anglos have been in the American desert landscape for about 150 years, a mere drop in the bucket of Gaian time. In the light of a Hopi perspective, that's just long enough to stumble in, look up, blink, and mutter, "What's that? Where am I?" We see deserts as places of Biblical exile where we wander to go mad or bring back revelations. Madness and revelation. During a quarter of a century of wandering Utah's deserts, I have encountered plenty of both.

THREE

LANDING ON THE RIM
OF THE GREAT BASIN

Driving north from the Sleeping Rainbow, I crossed over broad dry valleys, passed beneath the classically majestic Wasatch Range, and then veered off towards Tooele. We were job and house hunting, checking out an offer I had to be the Tooele County Librarian. Tooele, pronounced toowilla, was an hour west of Salt Lake City in that transition zone between the snow-capped alpine ecosystem of mountains that has made Utah a prime skiing destination and the vast basins and ranges of the Great Basin Desert.

A change was due. We were tired of serving the rich in the middle of slickrock Paradise. I was tired of explaining to my guest-ranch employees why customers who could casually drop hundreds of dollars for turquoise jewelry on their way out the door, forgot to leave tips for the kids who made their beds, cleaned their toilets, and served their food. I was tired of answering enthusiastic questions from guests over dinner about the "beautiful" geology and ecology they had just encountered on hikes and jeep tours, only to discover later how heavily invested they were in resort condo developments, or the sale of strip-mining machinery, or drilling for oil and gas, or on and on. One guest breathlessly described her encounter with a bighorn sheep one moment and then, within a minute, confided to me that the Vietnam War was "very good" for Rockwell where she worked near Los Angeles. She was in personnel management and had been firing quite a few long-time employees since peace broke out.

The rich could slide right by any contradiction or implication of their power and advantage. They were bright and stupid at the same time, worldly and insular at once. Although they had traveled and lived all over, they stayed at the same swank hotels and watering holes and they were familiar with each other's exclusive neighborhoods even when they lived a thousand miles apart. They shared the same lawyers, brokers, and doctors. They sent their children to the same prep schools and colleges, bought them the same cars for their birthdays, and often sent them to the same therapy programs when the affluence they bestowed on them was corrupting. They sat on the same boards of universities, hospitals, banks, corporations, and charities. They tended to be politically and intellectually incestuous, endlessly cross-fertilizing the same small set of rationales and arguments to justify their privilege that they had been wearing out since the days of the robber barons from whom some of them descended. They had seen much and learned little. I would never belong to their tribe and I needed a break from them.

Linda wanted to be a full-time mom. We had generous time to devote to Brian over the guest-free winter, but tended to pass him around, put him off, and fit him in during the tourist season. Brian was two years old and didn't know what other kids looked like—he only saw them in passing when we drove seventy miles to Richfield to buy groceries. Kids need clean air, but they also need a neighborhood with friends to play with and a community where they can learn to become social and civic beings. Finally, when Linda was pregnant again, we felt it was time to settle down, build a nest, and devote ourselves to being a family.

We weren't at all sure how this was done, but we suspected a small town setting and a steady job might be prerequisites. During our early vagabond phase, I had been a rug cutter, truck driver, teacher, and reporter. Linda had been a nurse's aide, live-in guardian, and craft store manager. Then, together, we managed a fishing lodge and cottages in Vermont and then ran a guest ranch. We had moved and hustled, moved and hustled, always looking for the next cool place to be. Now we were looking for a Norman Rockwell painting to inhabit.

Grantsville fit the bill. Sort of. It was a small and quiet town of a few thousand, nestled like a bucolic oasis in a wide valley of sage, juniper, and grass beneath the postcard-perfect Stansbury Mountains. The Great Salt Lake formed its northern boundary. Grantsville still retained its rural characteristics despite the nearby army depot and magnesium refinery that were the area's major employers. Kids still belonged to Four-H Club and raised small animals in backyard rabbit hutches, chicken coops, and sheep pens. On a summer Saturday, the loudspeakers from the rodeo grounds filled the evening air with distorted echoes. Open irrigation ditches along main streets still carried nourishing mountain runoff to surrounding pastures where cattle dotted the wide horizon. It seemed like everyone in town owned a horse.

Mostly Mormon, town residents seemed to be "salt of the earth" types who worked hard, lived simply, and were devoted to their large families. The town did not have zoning for much of its history, so neighborhoods tended to be a mix of old and young, middle class and poor. New expensive houses alternated with trailer courts. The lax country attitude was also reflected in the number of unkempt vacant lots and the numerous rusting auto bodies perched on cinder blocks and stranded in overgrown backyards. If weeds and pests are signs of civilization, Grantsville was very civilized. I had never seen such robust ragweed or so many fat grasshoppers.

The state's bookmobile program was built in the 1950s, a time when Utah was mostly rural. There were so many small and isolated villages with no financial means for building and operating "fixed-site" libraries, the kind of brick edifices Carnegie funded, that a more efficient method of delivering library service was required. Bookmobiles were the answer. Twenty-two of them peppered the state. Each had a headquarters that warehoused extra books and often got double use as a town library. That was the case in Tooele County where the bookmobile headquarters shared the Grantsville City Hall and was also an open library.

I had never encountered a bookmobile before I moved to Capitol Reef. There, I met the congenial and wise Doug Christensen who drove out of Richfield and all the way to Bullfrog Basin at Lake Powell, stopping in small burghs, ranches, and the national park along the way. Doug told me about the job in Tooele and it sounded like fun. I loved books, liked people, and the prospect of putting the two together was inviting. I could actually get paid to do what I considered favorite pastimes, browsing books and recommending them to others. Later I would get a master's degree in library and information science, but at the time there was no hard and fast requirement for being a bookmobile librarian. My guest-ranch experience said I was self-directed and could handle the public, my teaching experience spoke to my intellectual capacity for guiding others to information, and I had driven a truck when I lived in Germany. The State Library Division offered me the job. After surveying Grantsville, I took it.

In the beginning I rented the entire third floor of a rundown Victorian-era house on Main Street and commuted the five hours south to be with Linda and Brian on weekends. The old house was covered with a layer of talcum-fine dust that blew in from the desert and kept me up at night sneezing and coughing, but it only cost a dollar a night when I was there. Mildred, my elderly widowed landlady, did not need income but hungered for company and the protective presence of a man in the house after dark.

Eventually I found a modest house on the corner of Clark and Kearl. I bought it from the town mayor, a salty character who, as sheriff, had risked his life during the arrest of the two infamous killers described in Truman Capote's *In Cold Blood*. He had been removed from his post when he was caught illegally neutering dogs, so he ran for mayor. A few years later he was removed from that office when it was discovered he'd been secretly rounding up stray canines and shooting them at his farm on the edge of town. The Dead Dog Saloon on Main Street was named after the incident. I don't think he really disliked dogs but, in a town with so many small farm animals, unrestrained dogs were a menace. The town couldn't afford an animal control officer, a truck, and the fees for housing and putting away strays. Twenty-two caliber bullets were cheap and the mayor was willing, so he did it on his own as a generous civic gesture. He gave me a fair price for the house and was generous about letting us live there until our loan came through. We had a golden retriever then and we watched her very carefully.

We arrived in a big rental truck on a hot Sunday in October. Mormons don't work on the Sabbath but our neighbors, Ron and Liz Brown, were kind enough to overlook our spiritual transgression and offer us places at their table for Sunday dinner. We were late and had to unload the truck quickly and get it back to Salt Lake. There wouldn't be time to sit down and visit over a hot meal. Also, we smelled like a locker room after a basketball game and there wasn't enough time to clean up. Thanks but no thanks, we said, feeling like we had slighted our next door neighbors right off the bat. An hour later while we worked, the Brown family reappeared carrying a tray of sandwiches they had made for us to eat on the run, pie, and a pitcher of milk. We knew we had made the right decision. Carly was born in the spring. Neighbors showed up at our door each night for a week carrying hot meals for us. We realized that Grantsville is one of those last enclaves of American small-town living where neighbors like the Browns can become so close that the boundaries between families mix and blur until the terms "friend" or "neighbor" seem inadequate to convey the depth of affection and caring that is shared.

As the county bookmobile librarian, I soon got to know the county's diverse residents and the land they lived on. I drove a big truck loaded with a few thousand books around to schools, ranches, and little towns on the dry valleys and deserts of western Utah. My patrons included ranchers, miners, army depot workers, and school children. There were polygamists and Goshute Indians in Skull Valley, casino workers on the Nevada border in Wendover, and soldiers and scientists at Dugway Proving Grounds. My stops included a couple of two-room brick schools, a Pony Express monument, and a mostly ghost town called Ophir. All totaled, I served about six thousand people spread out across nearly seven thousand square miles of the Great Basin.

Those who travel from Utah to California are familiar with this mind numbing geographic expanse known as the Great Basin. It is usually described by drivers as a tedious ten-hour ordeal of straight-ahead driving, up one side of a basin to a pass in an island range of mountains and then a long glide down into the center of another basin, then up again, over and over. If the Great Basin was a song, it would be a combination of "The Bear Went Over the Mountain" and "A Hundred Bottles of Beer on the Wall." If it was a movie, it would be *Groundhog Day* with tumbleweeds. When Brigham Young stood on a foothill of the Wasatch Mountains looking over the Salt Lake Valley below and pronounced to his Mormon wagon train "This is the place," he might as well have said, "It's now or never." No doubt his scouts told him that beyond that last fertile valley lay a smaller one and then hundreds of miles of rock, sun, salt, sand, and sage until California. Unlike the canyonlands of the Colorado Plateau, the Great Basin's high deserts are unloved. More characteristic of our attitude towards deserts, the Great Basin was considered a vast "wasteland" and an immense and unfortunate barrier to westward migration.

The Great Basin is, however, coveted by the military which sees its vastness and unpopularity as opportunity. Within its confines are the Dugway Proving Grounds, which alone are the size of Rhode Island, and also Nellis Air Force Base, Hill Air Force Range, the Hawthorne Army Ammunition Plant, and the infamous Nevada Test Site. The Department of Energy is now getting into the same act of environmental sacrifice that has been well practiced by the military throughout the Cold War. Yucca Mountain has been designated and is being developed as the national repository for spent nuclear fuel.

Those who come to the Great Basin with open minds and active senses, however, see it differently. The Great Basin is a unique place of silence and solitude that owns a spare and stubborn beauty. When settlers asked "what is it good for?" they were looking through a lens shaped by a Cartesian worldview and its materialistic and utilitarian drives. They missed the point. We are still missing the point. Like all ecosystems, it is good for itself.

Depending on where you mark the transition from one ecosystem to the next, and depending on how you add up its fractal edges, the Great Basin is about 165,000 square miles large. That's larger than California. It encompasses all of Nevada and much of Oregon, Idaho, and Utah. It is high, most of its floor is over 4,000 feet above sea level with 160 small mountain ranges rising like islands from there. It is a desert with cold nights and hard winters.

Like all deserts, it is also hot and dry. Summer temperatures can climb over one hundred degrees Fahrenheit for days on end. There is scant rainfall and rivers are rare and thin. The Great Basin got its name from John Fremont who trudged many miles over it looking for a river that drained into the Pacific and concluded that he was experiencing a vast basin with only interior drainage. When water does spill from the sky, it tends to run and cut—the erosive patterns of flash floods carve the landscape. Once unyielding ground is cut, the scar stays. The baked and frozen hardpan still reveals the ruts made by wagon trains a hundred and fifty years ago.

To survive on such a dry steppe-like land, the predominant plants of the "desertshrub" ecosystem sink deep taproots and grow a rich web of lateral roots to absorb what little moisture is available. Many plants live in symbiosis with root fungi that use the nutrients from decaying plant debris and then make those goodies available again to the plant. Little is wasted in this "wasteland." Plants there are sturdy survivors, not colorful and flamboyant like their desert cousins, the saguaro in the Sonoran Desert or the Joshua tree in the Mojave.

Spring rain and snowmelt can create a tapestry of brilliant wildflowers and rocks can hold bright, even neon, lichens, but for the most part the Great Basin appears in pastels and muted tones. Mostly there is sagebrush, salt brush, rabbit brush, black brush, gray molly, and shad scale. There is rice grass, pepper grass, and mustard weed. Farmers grow alfalfa and hay—even the crops are plain. But the combinations of spare and open lines, whole horizons, and subtle earth tones can still be beautiful.

The Great Basin is another landscape that is outside our historical paradigm of wet beauty. It demands a patient and open eye to see it is far from empty. The shrubs nourish deer and antelope while sheltering abundant rabbits, rodents, snakes, and lizards that attract owls and hawks and eagles.

Hawks and owls come to town for the rodents that feed on barnyard grains and are frequently seen sitting on fence posts and telephone poles. I once counted ten golden eagles in a single tree near Vernon. Farther out on the desert, the mournful songs of coyotes can be heard at night—just what you'd expect. What might be surprising is the number of seabirds.

The Great Basin wasn't always dry. Only 10,000 years ago, an instant in geological time, Lake Bonneville covered about 20,000 square miles across what are now the western deserts of Utah. That's the size of Lake Michigan. Lake Lahontan to the northwest covered another 8,000 square miles. The level shorelines of Lake Bonneville are plainly etched along the slopes of the Oquirrh Mountains west of Grantsville. An enormous sand and gravel bar that rises between Tooele and the little town of Stockton to the south also offers mute testimony to a wet past. The remnants of the giant inland Pleistocene sea are also evident to the north where wetlands surround the Great Salt Lake. The lake itself concentrates the mineral legacy of ancient waters now gone.

Several million birds annually migrate along the shores of Great Salt Lake and nearby marshlands like those at Fish Springs southeast of Dugway. They include ducks, geese, swans, pelicans, avocets, sanderlings, killdeer, phalaropes, and whimbrels. You can find snowy egrets or snowy plovers, great blue herons and long-billed curlews. Gulls are ever present. In my earliest memories of gulls, they swarmed behind the roiling wake of the ferryboat that took us from Hoboken to Manhattan and competed for bits of garbage and small fish that were stirred to the surface. In the spring near Grantsville, I have often watched them make the same noisy airborne riot behind a tractor churning worms and bugs in its wake. Its seabirds are just one of the Great Basin's surprises. It is one of the few places on the planet where, if you were lucky, you could encounter a rattlesnake, a pelican, and a big horn sheep all on the same day.

Some of the Great Basin's secrets are a matter of distance. The Deep Creek Mountains, for example, are a seventy-mile trip from I-80 on gravel roads. From the gravel roads, four-wheel drive is required to get over the muddy rutted routes into mountain canyons. Those who invest and persist drive by herds of startled antelope and are rewarded with spectacular views of gnarly canyon walls, jagged snowy peaks, and twisted stands of thousand-year-old bristlecone pines. Few people do persist, mostly elk hunters. Even the trail to Ibapah Peak, probably the most popular in the range, is faded and overgrown. Smaller gems are also hidden deep within the Great Basin. I once swam in a pond-size hot spring in Diamond Valley that was surrounded by lush green vegetation and the sweet trill of a dozen different songbirds. It was like stumbling into a small corner of the Caribbean in the middle of a bone-dry lake bed. I could tell you how to get there but it's a day-long drive on dirt roads from any motel.

The Great Basin contains many smaller locally named deserts. The West Desert is that area, loosely named and located, that stretches away on either side of I-80 as you drive the ninety-eight miles from Grantsville to Wendover. There are no towns and there is no gas. It's a straight road. Most of the fatal accidents are rollovers when people fall asleep or forget to pay attention. Near Wendover are the snow-white salt flats that are still used to break land speed records. Mineral evaporation ponds and their canals have so impeded the natural rhythms of lakeside waters that the flats are thinning now and the glory days of testing out rockets on wheels may soon be over.

Much of the flat gray land along the highway looks like dry hardpan. There are no plants as far as you can see. It can look like cement and looks can be deceiving. Tourists passing through are sometimes tempted to veer off the highway for a spin on the wide flatlands of the desert. Invariably they are surprised when their vehicles break through the thin surface and become bogged in the dank mud below. Although the water table is that close to the surface, the water is a bitter brew for man or beast.

Pioneers had the same problem. On the corner of Clark and Hale in Grantsville sits the Donner-Reed Museum, filled with the flotsam and jetsam tossed overboard by those hapless settlers as they took a short cut through the West Desert, became mired in mud, and lost precious days getting to the Sierra. The rest, as they say, is history. Trapped in the Sierras by an early snowstorm, they starved and then carved each other up for food. It all started just west of town.

The West Desert was the wall the Mormon pioneers had their back up against after Joseph Smith was shot in Illinois and they fled across the plains. Rush Valley, where Tooele and Grantsville were settled, was the last stop before the wheel-sucking thirsty desert. It was entered just days after Brigham Young's party arrived in the Salt Lake Valley and settled a couple of years later in 1849. There were tall grasses, clear springs, and timber to be had. Eventually gold was discovered and a mini-rush ensued. The ghost towns of Mercur, Ophir, Jacob City, and Gold Hill were left behind when the rush was over, those and hundreds of dangerous open mine shafts that occasionally swallow foolish teenage adventurers or ATV riders who aren't paying attention. Following the attack on Pearl Harbor, the valley experienced a military boom when a 25,000 acre tract of land between Tooele and Grantsville was selected for the site of the Tooele Ordnance Depot. The mining and military booms attracted an ethnically diverse population but the county remained predominantly Mormon. The names of the original settlers sent by Brigham to colonize the valley and the names of my neighbors and library patrons often matched. The first whites came and stayed.

No matter how old their roots in the valley, my bookmobile patrons lived along the rim of the West Desert. The center of the West Desert is uninhabitable. When I moved there in 1978, county commissioners, state planners, and legislators were still in the chin-stroking stage, looking west and wondering "what good is it?" There was lots of brackish water right under the surface but it was not suitable for human or livestock consumption. The scant biosphere would hardly feed a cow, even by the low standards of the American West. The minerals that weren't already extracted were thin and unprofitable. Unlike Utah's Colorado Plateau with its necklace of national park jewels, this desert was not drawing tourists from New York and Germany.

It did draw soldiers. Just a few miles northeast of town was the Tooele Army Depot. I had passed the sign on the highway and immediately met people who worked there. It was the county's major employer. Most of those who described their jobs talked about degreasing, rebuilding, and then painting engines. That seemed innocent enough. Then I climbed one weekend to the top of Deseret Peak in the Stansbury's and looked down on the depot. What are all those lines of bumps that look like rivets, I asked naively? My hiking companion laughed in disbelief and then informed me I was looking at dozens of bunkers filled with munitions.

Our first spring, this became obvious in a big way. We were out on our lawn playing baby games with our kids when the house rattled and a thunderous boom followed. Alarmed, we ran to a neighbor and asked if she knew what had happened and wondered aloud if we should listen to the radio for news of some disaster. I expected to see helicopters descending with paramedics and bullhorns at any moment. Again, the response was bemusement. "They're just blowing up old bombs," she replied, "they'll be doing that every day until the fall." Bomb season. Sure enough, an hour later there was another boom and then another. Sure enough, you grow accustomed to it or just learn to swallow your anger.

Actually, it was more and less than bombs. Munitions of all kinds were stored in bunkers at the Tooele Army Depot and munitions, like groceries, go stale. They become unstable and have to be disposed. Taking the old stuff off the inventory and over to pits north of town and exploding them was the traditional means of disposal. Sometimes the explosions were small and hardly noticeable. Others threatened to crack plaster and glass. Dogs would bark, horses gallop in mad circles in their corrals, and babies would wake from naps and cry. Often, a huge dirt and smoke cloud would rise slowly up into the blue sky and then drift over town, leaving a fine dusting of dirt and who knows what on lawns, cars, gardens, and clothing hung to dry.

The military paved the way for private polluters. The Magcorp magnesium refinery north of town is arguably the dirtiest industrial operation in America. Magcorp leases about 100,000 acres of federal land next to the Great Salt Lake to use as lake water evaporation ponds. They collect the magnesium chloride that is left behind and submit it to a highly secret electrolytic process that splits the magnesium from the chloride. For every pound of magnesium thus produced, three pounds of free chlorine result. Magcorp spews out about 85 percent of the nation's total of point-source chlorine gas emissions and about 90 percent of Utah's total toxic pollution. Every year it tops the annual Toxic Release Inventory for total emissions, but its remote desert location lends the operation a kind of anonymity that would be envied by other polluting industries. On most days, it is noticeable as a mere plume on the horizon.

I first noticed Magcorp when we came home one night and smelled chlorine. It smelled like someone had broken a bottle of bleach in the street. Again, the call to a neighbor. "That's Magcorp," she said, "sometimes when the wind is just right, we get their stink."

"But it smells like bleach, not smoke," I protested.

"Haven't you ever smelled the bus from Magcorp when it comes through town?" she said. "All those guys wreak of chlorine." Shortly after, I realized that Magcorp workers did not park their cars near the town cemetery and catch a bus out to the plant because it was a long twenty-mile ride, but because the emissions from the factory were known to eat the paint off cars. "What does it do to lungs?" I asked another neighbor. My query was met with indifferent shrugs, as if the question was unusual and not important.

The people who live on the rim of the West Desert also express marginality in the way they live and what they accept.

Historically, scarcity has been the rule. By the 1930s, the tall grasses the settlers found were gone and overgrazed. Grantsville was in a mini Dust Bowl, surrounded by pits and dunes. Farming was next to impossible and the highway traffic running from Salt Lake in the east to California in the west didn't bring enough business to supply many jobs. When Tooele was selected for an army depot, far from the range of Japanese planes, the local populace rejoiced. Government jobs were secure jobs with good benefits. Even the depot's waste was welcome. Several Grantsville homes were constructed using cast-off ammo crates for lumber. The siting of Magcorp in the early postwar years was regarded as another clever coup.

"A bird in hand is worth two in the bush." "Don't look a gift horse in the mouth." "Ya dance with the one that brung ya." These are the mottos of a scarcity that leads to risk taking that would be unacceptable to those who are wealthier and more powerful. In Tooele County, for example, those who worked at the Tooele Army Depot, for years the county's major employer, routinely breathed paint fumes and solvents or were busy handling munitions, including chemical weapons. Those who worked at the Anaconda Mine, another major employer now closed, faced the dangers of underground mining. Those who work at Magcorp breathe chlorine. Those who work at the Kennecott smelter are exposed to arsenic and heavy metals. Workers at Dugway got extra pay for allowing mosquitoes infected with encephalitis to bite them in one of hundreds of experiments conducted there. If you ranch on the side, you also encounter pesticides and herbicides.

People in town complain, but only quietly to each other over backyard fences. Grantsville is a small and tight-knit town.

Lots of people owe their livelihood to Magcorp and the military. Among those who are not directly employed, everyone has relatives, or neighbors, or friends, or some combination of the above who work at Magcorp or an incinerator. We don't bite the hand that feeds us, or even bite the hand that feeds a neighbor, especially in a culture where that hand has been withdrawn time and again. People on the rim of the West Desert know what happens when mines close and crops fail. Bust and drought are always lurking on the edge of our emotional horizon.

Although the list of hazards kept growing as we became aware of our desert surroundings and the peculiar history of their occupation and use, we also could not escape the charm and beauty of the place. Most days the air is clear, skies are wide and blue, and the constant horizon is filled with postcard-pretty snow-capped mountains. The forested canyons and streams of the Stansbury Mountains are a fifteen-minute drive away. Cougars still show up in town in the winter, eating pets and perching on fence rails until they scare the bejeezus out of those who come across their bright eyes in the middle of the night.

So we stayed. Life was good. We had another baby, a boy we named Tyler, and our days were filled with love and laughter. Ours was not a normal home life, it was ideal. We focused inward towards the warm scenes and heartening experiences our family provided abundantly. It took an MX missile to get me to look up.

FOUR

MX MARKS THE SPOT

It was 1984, for real. George Orwell anticipated an all-powerful government that called war "peace". Beating ploughshares into swords was not far off. To the Congress, media, and much of the American public, Ronald Reagan, with his smooth-as-Teflon style and knowing wink at the camera, was a trusted and patriotic father and he was leading us into a new Cold War. For our own good, of course.

As it turned out, Big Brother had a mellifluous tone and a bottomless PR budget, all the better to convince us that free markets are free and that massive state intervention to stimulate the profits of Mr Reagan's California defense industry allies was really "getting government off our backs." The champions of free enterprise sold us socialism for the rich and laissez faire for the poor by successfully portraying a sclerotic Soviet Union on the verge of collapse as a robust Evil Empire worthy of a trillion-dollar defense build-up response. No doubt Kremlin elites also used the politics of fear and division to manufacture a consensus among Russians for an ongoing transfer of wealth and privilege to themselves, but in America in the eighties, the military sector had a feeding frenzy.

Reagan Republicans were elected on the premise that government didn't work and, once in office, they set out to prove it. That is, their regime worked quite well for some and badly for most. If you had lots of stock in Boeing, you had a lovely view out of Reagan's "window of vulnerability." If you were poor or mentally disabled, you landed on the street where you could look up at the holes in the "safety net" that Daddy Warbucks promised would catch you. If you were a young and common working taxpayer, you saw a mountain of national debt piling up on the horizon, obscuring the view you once had of your retirement years. If you were a rustbelt laborer, you saw your uncle's back in the unemployment line. If you were a peasant in Central America or tiny Grenada, you saw an empty plate and a gun labeled "democracy." But no matter where you stood, it all looked good on the TV.

In perfect Orwellian pitch, our collective paranoia was generated by "military intelligence," the suicidal accumulation of nuke missiles was for self-preservation, greed was good, and selfishness was touted as the cornerstone of citizenship. Thus, subsidy for the few became "security" for the many. Like the first Cold War, Cold War Two was very stimulating.

As usual, when Pentagon and Kremlin fat cats looked for a scratching post for newly acquired claws, they found a desert. In the Soviet Union it was in Kazakstan. In the United States, it was in my backyard. We were almost three years into our bucolic life in Grantsville when disturbing news began to appear about the extent to which the Great Basin was up for grabs and the willingness of the Pentagon to turn it into a military environmental sacrifice zone.

A few years before, in 1979, work was begun on the MX

missile. It was designed to replace or augment our current Armageddon war-horse, the Minuteman missile. The MX would be very big. Each one would stand seventy feet erect and weigh 192,000 pounds. Each would carry ten warheads so powerful and accurate they could penetrate and destroy Soviet missile defenses or any other "hardened" target, like underground command centers. If the US launched a pre-emptive MX strike against the Soviet Union, they might not have many missiles left to fire back. However, since it was counter to US strategy to launch a first strike, they were referred to as having "second-strike ICBM countersilo capability." "Silo busters," for short.

What was most remarkable about the missile was not its fat firm size or ability to find a target and penetrate, but the way it would be deployed. Some 200 multiple warhead missiles, 2,000 warheads in all, would be hidden under 4,600 shelters scattered across the desert floor of the Great Basin. It was to be a classic "shell game" scenario with each missile being a 192,000-pound pea and each shelter a potential shell. Shells would be arranged in clusters along "racetracks." Real missiles and dummy missiles on massive transporters would dart from shell to shell. By constantly moving all the missiles and dummies around, the ol' Ruskies would have to guess which of the pods the nuclear pea was under. Chances were, they would have to target all the shells to be sure they'd hit the ones that counted, thus further draining the Evil Empire's resources and accelerating the game of military/economic chicken we were playing.

The Devil, as usual, was in the details. Constructing such a basing mode would cost at least $100 billion, in 1980 dollars. About 8,500 miles of roads or rails would be built from shell to nuclear shell. That's the distance from Maine to California and back again. These wouldn't be your normal interstate highway type of roads or Amtrak rail lines either. They would have to be able to withstand the massive weight of MX missiles and their transporters. Figuring that a mile between shelters would be required for maximum effect, construction of racetracks and shelters would cover 15,000 square miles. Support and security facilities would expand the needed area to about 40,000 square miles. That's the size of Vermont, Massachusetts, New Hampshire, Connecticut, and Rhode Island. Altogether, the MX missile system would have been the biggest construction project in American history—bigger than the Panama Canal or the Alaskan pipeline.

The impact on the Great Basin can only be described in hyperbole. The water that would be used for cement and sucked up by thirsty construction workers was estimated at 42 billion gallons. To build and then operate the system for twenty years, about 190 billion gallons of water would be required. The Great Basin, of course, is a desert. All available water would go to the project. Wells would have to be driven deep into aquifers which would certainly drop drastically and might even run out.

Estimates of needed water did not include dust suppression. The soils of the Great Basin are dry and powdery. Wind is frequent, if not constant. The prospect of thousands of bulldozers, graders, trucks, and other kinds of heavy equipment criss-crossing thousands of square miles of desert during the construction period raised the specter of historically unprecedented dust clouds and air pollution. One hundred million tons of aggregate would also have to be dug up, leaving the land permanently at the mercy of wind erosion. Visibility at the region's national parks, including the Grand Canyon, would be drastically reduced.

Although the area would boom temporarily with the need to build fifteen construction camps to house 50,000 workers, after the boom, in the classic western tradition, there would be a more or less permanent bust. Security and control needs would eliminate mining and grazing within the vast MX range. Hunting would be out of the question, as would be small planes and jeeps full of rockhounds and sightseers. Local governments would have to defer to military officers who would command the area's resources and be positioned to veto any local plan that did not fit into the larger security needs of the missile range. The natural environment, local economy and culture, and democracy itself would all have to stand before the MX firing squad.

As the mind-boggling plan unfolded, I was lifted from my Little House on the Prairie complacency to guard the precious nest Linda and I had been weaving around our children. I called around and put together about two dozen friends and neighbors, including the local Catholic priest, to form the Tooele County Anti-MX Coalition. I think we met once at our house and decided to write letters and make phone calls to the governor and our Congressional representatives. We really didn't know what we were doing but we knew we had to try something.

I remember handing out copies of a page I had found in the Quaker *Friend's Journal*. The eight-inch by ten-inch page was covered with a grid consisting of about a hundred squares. The squares, in turn, were covered with 6,000 little dots. In the center of the grid was a square that was empty except for a single dot. The text below the grid explained that the solitary center dot represented all of the firepower expended in all of World War Two, about 3 megatons in total. Each of the other 6,000 dots also represented 3 megatons of firepower. Taken together, they added up to 18,000 megatons of destructive power, the amount that was currently available to the US and the USSR. In other words, the combined nuclear arsenal of the two Cold War superpowers equaled the potential firepower of 6,000 World War Twos. A single Poseidon submarine, the text went on to explain, contained firepower equal to three World War Twos. The US had thirty-one such subs and ten similar Polaris subs. We also had new Trident subs with the firepower of eight World War Twos each. "Place a dime on the chart," urged the text, "and the covered dots represent enough nuclear destructive power to destroy all the large and medium sized cities in the entire world. What are you going to do with the rest of your coins?"

If the MX deployment scheme seemed crazy, it was a madness that emerged within the context of an even greater madness, the Cold War. That insanity was willing utterly to sacrifice a Western desert area the size of New England to military preparedness for an Armageddon none of us could long survive. I lived on the rim of that potential sacrifice zone. I hadn't heard the word ecocide yet, but I knew that was what I was looking at.

If you think "environmental sacrifice zone" is hyperbole, that surely a multistate area the size of the Great Basin would not be sacrificed in such a way, then go look for the Great Plains. A vast area of America where the buffalo once roamed is now reduced to a patchwork of "remnants," small leftover plots containing colorful collections of wildflowers and diverse native grasses, hidden among the vast expanses of farmland. Long ago, the leaves of grass were replaced by amber waves of grain. That, and endless geometric rows of corn and soybeans. You can drive for days in the Midwest and see nothing but Monsanto green. The quaint farms we see in Dorothy's knocked-out dream of Oz have been replaced with the vast holdings of agribusiness powers. As Aunty Em was replaced by ADM, the trend towards taking the ducks and pigs out of the barn and replacing them with even more chemically induced monoculture has intensified. As movingly described by Sandra Steingraber in *Living Downstream*, there is a price for losing diversity. Heavy chemical management is required. As a result, Midwest rivers get loaded with fertilizer runoff and citizens walk down Main Street with atrazine in their veins. And we take all of this for granted. If we could clear the buffalo from the plains and replace them with grain silos, then we could clear the antelope from the desert and replace them with missile silos. Is food that much more elemental than fear? Or, as I would later learn, if the Great Plains can be cleared to make the nation's breadbasket, then why couldn't the Great Basin become the nation's wastebasket? We need bread and we need a place to dump our toxic trash or try out weapons and hide them.

Our Utah senator at the time was Jake Garn, later famous for donating a kidney to his daughter and vomiting in outer space. Jake wanted the missile but not the basing mode. He didn't think the voters understood the distinction between his case of missile envy and his reluctance to draw a bull's eye on Salt Lake's Temple Square. So, he invited opponents of the MX in for a chat.

We were an odd collection, ranging from old hippie peaceniks to a retired admiral. The admiral had been a Pentagon big-shot and also wanted the missile system but was against the basing scheme, probably for the unstated reason that the navy also wanted a piece of the MX pie and racetracks on the desert left them out. The admiral was clearly uncomfortable being associated with the ragged entourage in Garn's office. He had trouble making eye contact with us and seemed visibly embarrassed when we spoke.

At one point, as the conversation dragged on, a young woman exclaimed that she didn't see why we needed the missile at all, period, what with all the ones we already had. Wasn't this foolish and suicidal? The admiral jumped at the chance to display his hawkish inclinations. No, he rebuked her, the missile was necessary, it just needed to be deployed differently. Yes, added Senator Garn, if she could only see the intelligence reports that he was privy to, she would understand the Soviets were dangerous and could not be trusted. The admiral one-upped the Senator. "If you want to know what the Soviets are up to," he said, "read the *Communist Manifesto* by Marx and Lenin where the entire Soviet plan for world conquest is outlined." Garn quickly and enthusiastically agreed.

I was shocked. My jaw actually dropped. Up until then I had been quiet, too unsure of myself to speak up. But I knew some history and they had it all wrong. "Wait a minute," I heard myself stammer, "the *Communist Manifesto* was written in 1848 by Marx and Engels. Lenin hadn't even been born. It's an analysis of labor–capital relations in nineteenth-century Europe and how marketplace dynamics shape behavior. It is visionary because it anticipates a global economy but it isn't a blueprint or handbook. There is no mention of the Soviet Union because it didn't exist and Russia was the last place they figured there would be a revolution."

The admiral and Garn looked mortified, the room fell silent, and then I turned red. Someone changed the subject and we all backpedaled from the awkward space we had fallen into. As the meeting in the senator's Salt Lake office dispersed, I was feeling flabbergasted and discombobulated. Alligators wrestled and clawed in my belly as I realized the implication of my encounter. I could no longer rationalize my failure to speak up and act with the notion that smart people are in charge. A cantankerous future loomed.

I was not naive. A power elite that was willing to sacrifice my generation for dubious purposes in Vietnam was certainly capable of ecocidal schemes on unloved American deserts, and I had no illusions about the benevolence and competence of the government, but I still assumed they operated somewhere within the ballpark of reality. I assumed my foes were wrong but rational. They may be conditioned by a culture of acquisition to be insensitive and brutally self-interested, as Marx had argued in the famous book the senator and admiral misunderstood, but they were not suicidal and stupid. As I left Garn's office that day, I was shaken to realize the world was governed by fear and fantasy, as if traumatized amnesiacs had taken control. It was nuts. We, the people of the whole wide world, were stuck in the back seat of a speeding car engaged in a game of nuclear chicken with Curly, Moe, and Larry in the driver's seat.

The encounter in Senator Garn's office was a turning point. I realized even common citizens like myself, a rural librarian at the time, could have valuable insights and knowledge to bring to public discussions and decisions. I resolved to listen to my doubts, learn more, keep an open mind, think twice, and be honest about what I don't know, but to never ever hesitate to express my concerns and convictions again.

The MX basing scheme was eventually thrown out. Too expensive. Not enough of the boondoggle pie for a Navy that wanted a sea-based deployment. Although the relative handful of active and vocal MX opponents can share the credit for bringing the behemoth down, most credit goes to the Church of Jesus Christ of Latter Day Saints. Eventually the Church came out against the Pentagon's pea in the pod plan. Apparently, the old men in the Mormon Church's world headquarters tower in Salt Lake City did not fancy living next to a Soviet nuclear missile magnet. Placing the heart of the Mormon population directly in the rocket sights of the Soviets did not jive with existing revelation. As I would learn later, Mormons had already been downwind from atomic fallout. No doubt most of the Church's leaders had family members, friends, or neighbors who had cancer. They might be loyal, stoic, and silent about the first waves of lethal radiation sent their way, a chance to show America that they should not be set apart because of their controversial polygamist past, but there are limits to what can be expected and endured. MX crossed the line.

The separation of church and state in Utah is not like the wall it is elsewhere in the nation, but more like a veil. Utah politicians and voters stand ready to be pulled through that veil whenever LDS Church leaders even wink or nod at them. Church leaders are not explicit about the political outcomes they favor, but are as adept at sending subtle messages to their flock as the brethren are at receiving them. For the Church to come out against something means 70 percent of the Utah electorate has not only a clear sanction to oppose it, but is encouraged to do so. The MX was dead meat in Utah. The Church's influence, of course, extends far beyond Utah. They have rich resources and loyal followers across the country. The opposition of the powerful Church was a welcome coup de grace to the MX basing mode.

Although the MX bullet was dodged, the Cold War gunman was still at large and stalking the deserts of the West. It was plain to see. Political leaders who could contemplate turning my backyard into an apocalyptic labyrinth could not be trusted. I would soon find out there was a powerful precedent for sacrificing the desert environment and public health for military ends. It had happened before and my backyard was already well on its way towards being a sacrifice zone. The MX controversy was just a particularly sharp spike in a well-established pattern of abusive military activity on America's deserts. Once your eyes are open, it's amazing what you see.

FIVE

BREAKFAST CEREAL FOR
TWO-HEADED BABIES

The Lion's Hall in Grantsville has seen better days. Constructed of plain gray cinderblocks, the modest square structure sits on Main Street, across from the elementary school. It shares a corner lot with an abandoned post office building, now used to store the town's Christmas decorations, and with an aging firehouse that sits behind it. Its small front lawn is threadbare and weedy. Paint peels from the eves and the shingles are loose on the roof. In the spring of 1992 it was used for cheap wedding receptions, karate and clogging classes, and occasionally for public meetings.

I was sitting on an uncomfortable folding chair there, ready to listen and try to understand what was happening on the desert west of town. A vast West Desert Hazardous Industries Area (WDHIA) had recently been created on the rim of the eastern rim of the Great Basin to accommodate a burgeoning hazardous waste industry. Corporate America was no longer allowed to toss its toxic trash into the air or into the nearest moving water. Each year, millions of tons of toxic waste had to be disposed. Thousands of sites contaminated with polychlorinated biphenyls (PCBs), radiation, and various dangerous chemicals before environmental laws and policies were in place had to be cleaned up. Cleaned up often meant moved. The nation needed a rug to sweep its dirt under and the West Desert fit the bill. It was a damn big rug, outa sight and outa mind, with few buyers and fewer defenders. Spanish Conquistadors supposedly buried treasure in a hundred secret places in the desert that feverish searching has not revealed. How hard could it be to hide hazardous waste that no one wanted to find?

Tooele County commissioners, seeing that their desert backyard was going to be targeted for incinerators, decided to jump on the burning bandwagon and turn an otherwise "useless" piece of real estate into a money maker. They realized they could collect big impact fees by siting, out-of-sight, pariah businesses that had been turned down by a hundred other communities. The legislature would sweeten the pot for the customers by setting fees low in the high desert. Grab a big enough share of the hazardous waste market, they reasoned, and you can still generate profits, jobs, and revenues. The more waste the better as they translated pollution into jobs and revenue. Few cared for jackrabbits and salt brush, but everyone wanted a better future for their kids.

Two of the first tenants of the zone would be hazardous waste incinerators. At the time, they were referred to as the Aptus and USPCI incinerators. The USPCI operation, a subsidiary of Union Pacific, was eventually bought by Laidlaw and then Safety Clean as the haz-waste corporations jockeyed for position, consumed one another, and merged while sorting out winners and losers in the volatile new industry. Laidlaw eventually bought the spanking new Aptus incinerator to close it down and eliminate it as a competitor in the tight haz-waste incineration market. Tracking the changes in such an incestuous and cannibalistic arena is a kaleidoscopic experience.

The corporate reps and their PR advance team arrived at the Lion's Hall in smooth suits and fresh haircuts that seemed odd and out of place in such a worn and paltry setting. They smiled as they passed out slick brochures with bold headings that read "sharing," "solving," and "caring." The PR literature always emphasized that all of us generated hazardous waste and someone had to deal with the mess we made. Utah's temporary Democratic Congressman, Wayne Owens, warned that we were opening the state to waste we did not, in fact, generate and would be ill advised to accept. His voice was lost behind those of local government officials looking for an unexpected boom from a barren stretch of desert and those of the glad-handing PR consultants promising a "leading edge" industry. I sat on my metal chair and thumbed through USPCI's literature, looking up occasionally to see who in town was filing in and finding their places. People caught each other's eyes, exchanged greetings, and shared news the way residents of small towns do. I looked down and read about USPCI's "stirling reputation" for "responsible" hazardous waste disposal.

During the 1990s, more than two hundred proposed incinerators were defeated by opponents in communities where they were planned. Tooele County, however, was fertile ground. The new hazardous waste zone was largely welcome. Finally, someone had figured out what that worthless ground was good for. The county had tried for a long time to find a lucrative use for its West Desert real estate. In the mid-1960s, a giant 40-thousand-acre spaceport for the shuttle program was proposed.

Edwards Airforce Base got the landing site. In 1987, the county made a bid for a $6 billion "super-conducting collider," a fifty-two-mile ring of gigantic underground magnets to explore the substructure of atoms. Texas got it. Then there was a proposed electronic battlefield and then a giant gravitational wave observatory.

We had a tradition of trading environmental quality for jobs and revenue. County officials practically invited Magcorp to build on the rim of the desert despite its polluting potential. Local officials welcomed Dugway and the Tooele Army Depot when they lurked on to the scene. Nary an eye was batted over the placement of almost half of the nation's chemical weapons stockpile at TAD. Facilities to receive the nation's toxic waste were an easy step along the well-established path of economic development. Although putting the sons and daughters of miners to work in moon suits at the local hazardous waste dump hardly struck me as progress, I understood that the county's traditional standards for what is a "good job" were low. A good job was one that paid enough to keep the roof up and the kids fed. Lately, shiny pick-up trucks, motorcycles, and ATVs were being added to the list of what a good job brought. Benefits, of course, were important. As for security, it was largely unknown outside employment at the army depot.

The West booms and busts. Even the local restaurants and gas stations that once thrived from the Interstate traffic that came through town, died when the present I-80 was rerouted and constructed on the edge of the Great Salt Lake to the north. They were mostly empty now, except for the intermittent renters who would try to start something up, fail, and close shop. An old variety store hung on by carrying crafts on consignment and catering to after-school candy addiction. Each afternoon at three o'clock, hundreds of children bubbled out the doors of the elementary school across the street and made a beeline to the brightly colored sweets piled into old glass cabinets. The store was once used as a movie set for a story that required a Depression-era look and feeling. There were other stores in town that had the look, but they were falling apart and covered in bindweed. We were overdue for some boom.

If the desperation that accompanies scarcity left us open and vulnerable to those who would sell us a bill of goods, Utah's other Achilles heel is a local culture that mixes righteous patriarchal attitudes with blind faith in free enterprise. We are a straightforward society of hammers, guns, and gold horns, designed to build and prosper, acquire and profit. We do not regard industry and the military critically or skeptically, we embrace them. As long as good ol' boys are in charge, the imperative to defend property rights against allcomers will be a top priority. We don't need any pointy headed outsiders telling us we can't use our land any damn way we please.

Incineration itself was new to me. I tried to keep an open mind but it didn't make sense. I knew from high-school physics that you couldn't destroy matter, only transform it. If, as incineration proponents said, hardly any emissions came out the smokestack, then where did the bad stuff go? The answer, I learned, was that an inflated waste stream goes out the incinerator back door. Ash, brines, salts, metals, laboratory waste, filters, scrubber packing and so on all have to be buried as hazardous waste in amounts that often are several times the volume of waste burned. No wonder, then, that the lead state agency regulating incinerators was not the Division of Air

Quality, as one might expect, but the Division of Solid and Hazardous Waste. As I listened, incineration seemed to me like a very expensive and complicated way of treating hazardous waste. Still, I had lived on the West Coast and in the East and had seen firsthand how we used to deal with our obnoxious waste by dumping it directly into rivers or the ocean. This method seemed better than that. I didn't like it in my backyard, but I had to admit I had a large backyard.

The corporate scientist explained to the audience that this would be a "state of the art" incinerator, a term I would later compare with "cutting-edge ocean dumping." "When we finish treating this waste," he claimed, "you could spread it on your breakfast cereal and eat it." On the other side of the room was a Greenpeace activist from San Francisco who became increasingly alarmed at the engineer's soothing jargon-loaded descriptions and his unwillingness to acknowledge harm or risk from the proposed incinerator's emissions. By the time it was his turn to speak he was agitated.

Most of the audience had never heard the terms "dioxin" or "carcinogenic." We couldn't even muster intelligent questions. A mostly native Mormon crowd, they had an inherent suspicion of anyone from San Francisco, let alone a long-haired guy from Greenpeace in San Francisco. They respected science and technology. They wanted jobs and revenue. They liked good news. Pie in the Sky is more appealing than Love Canal. The Greenpeace guy was aware of their biases and his considerable disadvantage in making his points. In his desperate zeal, he overstated his case. "If you let USPCI incinerate upwind from you," he seemed to be warning, "you're all gonna end up giving birth to two-headed babies and die."

I believe the audience suspected the truth was somewhere in the middle but there was no one to help us sort it out. Most people can recognize unwarranted claims made out of self-interest, like "incineration is perfectly safe," but they also resent attempts to manipulate them through fear. I left the Lion's Hall that afternoon feeling frustrated. Why wasn't anyone helping us figure this out so we could make some informed choices? Isn't it the role of government regulators to get us beyond discussions of breakfast cereal for two-headed babies?

I was naive. Bureaucrats don't touch such controversial stuff because it causes stress, work, and hard choices. Say the wrong thing and you risked a brief career. Many plan to leave government employment while they are still young enough to take better paying jobs with the industries they once regulated. They are not going to initiate or even facilitate uncomfortable dialogues between business and the public on the future of the species, ours or any other, unless they are required to. Technical issues are hard to explain to a populace that is, for the most part, only semi-literate in science. Budgets and staff are stretched too thin as it is. Meanwhile, our elected representatives, who don't understand such complicated issues better than their constituents, are too busy pursuing hot button issues like pornography on the Internet or partial birth abortions to look at difficult technical choices and their implications.

The context for such issues is also difficult to understand. The environmental law and policies that apply are known by their acronyms, like NEPA (National Environmental Policy Act, pronounced Neepa) and RCRA (Resource Conservation and Recovery Act, pronounced Rickra), and are not well known or often explained to those who attend public hearings.

Until I became immersed in environmental issues, Neepa and Rickra could have been the names of ticket agents at the Calcutta Airport for all I knew. The underlying message conveyed by business and government alike, however, was clear: all of this is tightly controlled to ensure compliance and the government is looking out for you. So, don't worry. All is well.

Leaving the Lion's Hall that day with my neighbors and friends, Sandy and Rick Covello, who were transplants from California, I wondered aloud if we could find our way to a productive discussion. "Where is the middle ground?" A few days later, I had a plan. I realized the creation of the West Desert Hazardous Industries Area assumed incinerators would be part of the mix. Incineration on the West Desert was a done deal. The hearings were conducted to comply with the law and get us citizens to buy-in. The big decisions were made and now we could comment. What we really needed was some accountability beyond lip service and dog'n'pony shows.

My brother-in-law Bill had moved north from Capitol Reef and was working as an air monitoring scientist with a Salt Lake firm that was in touch with state and local officials who might acquire their services and expertise. Bill told me that the state, county, and feds were arguing over which of them was responsible for air monitoring. If the squabble continued much longer, the incinerators would be emitting pollution before monitors could get an accurate reading of what was currently in our air. Here, I thought, is the means to a middle ground. I talked the editor of the local newspaper into letting me write a guest editorial urging the government agencies to get going soon on building an air monitoring system that could give us a clear profile of our air "before" and "after" incineration. That way we would have a basis for comparison and could tell what impact incineration was having on the quality of the air we breathe. I also asked for a health study so we would have a baseline for comparing health before and after.

In retrospect, I did not understand how complicated, expensive, and ambiguous air monitoring and epidemiological studies could be. Apparently, lots of other folks in the county were just as naive. Sandy started a petition drive asking for air monitoring and a health study. She expected to get about fifty signatures, enough to take to the newspaper, state agencies, and county commissioners as evidence that others shared my opinion. In two weeks, she got 500 signatures. The effort burst out of her hands as people reprinted the petition and gathered signatures on their own. She was sure she never kept track of or collected all of them.

Clearly, we had struck a nerve. The conventional wisdom at the time was that local people were apathetic about environmental issues. What happened? Sandy had no doubt. Over and over she heard stories, frightening stories, about cancer and chronic illness. People in Grantsville, she was told, are sick and dying and no one is paying attention.

This news came abruptly and was a shock. Sure, we were aware of dangers on the periphery of our pastoral community, but I was more concerned that my boys would tease a bull or trip over barbed wire than encounter carcinogens. It is a challenge for the parents of exuberant children to digest the usual fears, like cars, kidnappers, fire, and falling, without adding sinister and mysterious illness to the brew of parental concerns. We got up each day and tried to live joyously in the moment. We focused on the good in our lives. Like all parents, the logistical load of homework, ball games, piano lessons, hikes, picnics, errands, and earaches left us little time to worry about much beyond our roof and yard. Bogged down by the paraphernalia and limitations of children, we stuck close to home, played games on the lawn, planted a garden. Spare time was kid time. The world, even that of Tooele County's towns and facilities, seemed removed and distant.

Once Sandy tuned me on to them, I heard the stories about illness, too, and not just in Grantsville. Up and down the county line, it seemed like everyone along the rim of the West Desert had a sad tale to tell. It was bigger than that. Everyone I met who had lived along the rim of the entire Great Basin could click off a list of friends, neighbors, and family members who had cancer.

Why hadn't we noticed this before our petition? People were willing to talk about their health problems but they did not announce them on their own. Illness is a family affair, intimate really, and is usually shared with a trusted few, as are tears, and sorrow, and doubt. The bad news was masked by pride, one household at a time.

The Covellos, like us, had moved to Grantsville to raise their girls in a clean and wholesome setting. We had considered ourselves devoted and wise parents. Suddenly our faith in our decision-making abilities was shaken. Our judgement was in doubt. Had we inadvertently put our children in harm's way? A stain was spreading across our positive view of life in Grantsville and an investigation was in order.

We knew that small towns operate on anecdote. Every rumor had at least three versions. We knew that the more you look for something, the more you see it, until it looms large in your perspective. That's the nature of perception and consciousness. But when you realize that there is cancer in every third house you pass, the evidence becomes compelling. While walking through the cemetery at the end of my street one bright afternoon, I noticed that I was familiar with many of the names etched in stone and scattered among the lilacs. They were not just the names of old people and I had not been living in Grantsville very long. Two women on our street in their thirties had succumbed to cancer and were buried there.

Over the next several weeks, the various government agencies agreed to our requests and started to cooperate. We were assured that a "state of the art" air monitoring system would go up and soon. We got our way on that but it was cold comfort. I was worried. I needed answers about the health of my community. I asked the state for help but my concerns were met by bureaucrat scientists in Salt Lake with the kind of condescending disdain scholars have for old wives and their tales. Health studies are very expensive, I was told, and we don't undertake them on the basis of rumor and anecdote. Scientists are important people who cannot just drop their work and head out to every neighborhood where panic breaks out. Clearly, people in baseball caps adorned with the logo of the local hardware store were not supposed to set the agenda for scientists and their government colleagues.

The following spring, in 1993, I was offered a chance to attend a conference in San Diego sponsored by the Agency for Toxic Substance and Disease Registry, always called by its acronym ATSDR. Clinton had just been elected and the staff at ATSDR was seeing daylight for the first time in years. The Reagan/Bush regime, elected on the premise that government doesn't work, often fulfilled its own prophecy, especially as it concerned environmental regulation. Agencies like ATSDR had suffered under hostile political administrators, tight budgets, and crippling constraints. Now they were inviting people who lived near military installations across the country, an obvious stakeholder group for an agency dealing with environmentally induced illness, to come to San Diego and tell them how they could do better. I was invited because I was noticed as someone who could split the difference between the two-headed baby crowd and those who would serve them breakfast. I was articulate. ATSDR even paid my way.

In San Diego I met the walking wounded of the military's war on the environment. As I arrived at the hotel and mixed with the conference participants who were gathering in the hotel lobby, I was struck by what an odd and varied group they were. The environmental activists I was used to seeing were the ones I saw at hearings and rallies about wilderness issues, like grazing in desert canyons. Those people were close to the stereotype of tree huggers. They were fit and natural folks, the kind who eat granola and organic vegetables, shun cosmetics, work out, and buy their clothes from LL Bean. They spend serious time and energy hiking, biking, boarding, birding, rafting, kayaking, and otherwise communing with the big outdoors. They speak eloquently about the spiritual aspects of their favorite outdoor activities. I relate to them easily. But this was another side to the environmental movement I had not seen, and as I was arriving at the hotel in San Diego, it was carrying its luggage into the lobby. And that baggage included not a few oxygen tanks and wheelchairs. Many of these folks wore polyester and their luggage was worn out and cheap. There was little leather and much plastic. Many of them were red, black and brown. These were the folks who lived near the more than 20,000 toxic waste sites identified on military property and they or their loved ones and neighbors were sick. That's why they were there. The spirituality of wild places had nothing to do with it. One look at them and it was clear that environmental issues are about who has power and how that power is employed. They don't build chemical weapons incinerators in Aspen. I met no activists named Winfield or Muffy.

Talking to the conference participants over the next few days and asking how they got involved was heartbreaking. Most had never been politically active before their health was shattered or they watched a loved one suffer or die. Each had a different tale to tell but their stories had a common theme— illness. They described stillbirths, miscarriages, birth defects, blood disorders, cancer, and chronic ailments that could not be diagnosed. Often whole extended families were devastated by disease. One Hispanic woman had lost aunts, uncles, cousins, a parent, and a child to a rare blood disorder. Another young woman told me that she had two normal children by easy births before she moved near a military base. After the move, she had a stillbirth and then gave birth to a boy with serious disabilities.

As they found others in their communities who were also suffering, the walking wounded sought the advice of medical experts. Epidemiologists could not agree. In studies they suspected were inconclusive by design, their problems were attributed to genetics or personal behaviors, like having sex too early in life, poor diet, or smoking. Often, a community's problems were dismissed as a "statistical anomaly" or clouded because of "invalid sample size."

The civilian walking wounded of the Cold War were a subset of a larger population of techno-victims and disappeared against a broader background of cancer and illnesses that are woven through the fabric of western civilization at the close of the twentieth century. We'd been poisoning ourselves and rerouting our chromosomes for decades with everything from DDT to thalidomide. I've heard more than one epidemiologist say, "If you live long enough, you're bound to have cancer." The walking wounded thought of themselves as exceptions, but scientists and doctors told them they were the rule.

One by one, these plain folks, trusting and patriotic, discovered that the trail from their sickbeds led directly to the military's gates. Usually it was solvents, fuels, and other toxic chemicals that had leaked into groundwater. Sometimes it was radiation or other potent emissions that had drifted over homes and crops. In many cases, the causes of their suffering were demonstrable and clear because the pathways of pollution were obvious and the bodily results matched what you would expect from the specific exposures. Most of the times, however, the military was able to avoid liability because there were other complicating and clouding exposures. For example, a farmer with cancer whose drinking water has been contaminated by the military might also have a history of exposure to pesticides and herbicides. In another case it might be asbestos or lead paint from an old building where one once lived, solvents or PCBs encountered at work, and on and on.

The fact that we are routinely exposed to so many environmental health hazards complicates the search for causes and solutions, but it makes accountability even more problematic. For example, are so many Gulf War vets ill today because of inoculation shots they got before they left for the front, or was it the stress of being in a combat zone that did them in? Did exposure to insecticides cause illness? How about exposure to clouds of nerve gas drifting around after Saddam's bunkers were detonated? What about radiation from the depleted uranium munitions that we used to penetrate Iraqi tanks, or toxic smoke from oil well fires? The answer, of course, is that so many Gulf War vets are sick because of some or all of the above and more. Not only did sources and doses vary for each soldier, but the ability of individual soldiers to cope with exposure was affected by age, physical conditions, behaviors, states of mind, and so on. And those factors can all vary over time, too. The same is true for all of us. The hazards we encounter are many and our ability to cope with exposure is variable.

How do you sort it all out with certainty? You can't. The human body is not a math problem with decimal points that can be manipulated. It is a fluid creature in a fluid environment. That's the reality. But our world is organized around hard measures, fixed laws, and rules of evidence. Even when the empirical case could be made, however, it was hard to make it. The walking wounded were caught in a Catch-22 dilemma. Government scientists and doctors would not agree to undertake a community health study without hard evidence to justify their investment, but without a health study there was only anecdotal evidence to go on. Because of the broad and inclusive nature of health, the evidence that is available can consistently accumulate and yet never quite add up to proof, and the burden of proof is not on those who pollute but on those who encounter and incorporate it.

The military never missed a chance to avoid responsibility. If an individual with cancer had lots of family members with the same disease, then the military would claim the illness was hereditary. This was particularly aggravating to one young woman I met at the conference who claimed her extended family had a history of cancer but they also shared the same environment and hazardous exposures. Genes are not all that families have in common, she told me, we also share environments. In her family's case, she argued, widespread cancer might have nothing to do with genes and everything to do with proximity. When genetic predisposition to cancer was clear, it was always treated as the one and only cause, even though predisposition simply means you are more susceptible to cancer, not fated to have it. Environmental factors can be crucial in determining who among the genetically vulnerable actually gets it. Claiming that heredity is the sole cause of cancer when there are also lots of hazardous environmental exposures to consider is a lot like flooding a locked room with six feet of water and then claiming that people in the room drowned because they were short.

The hazards from military activities varied, but the denial, cover-ups, and resistance to accountability were always the same. During the Cold War, we gave the US military an exemption from democracy. They played by different rules, their own rules, or no rules at all behind tall walls and guarded gates. Such barriers are hard to breach. A culture of secrecy developed that meant hiding the truth was habitual and they didn't take notes.

Also, the military accepts casualties. You cannot take a hill from the enemy without losing troops. Commanding officers have a hard time understanding the complaints of mere civilians who are not feeling well. Suck it in, they seemed to say, and get on with it. And finally, the environment was simply not a priority. Winning the Cold War was the compelling goal supported by a clear popular consensus. Just as in Vietnam a village might be burned in order to save it, our environment was sacrificed to protect our way of life.

The walking wounded were vulnerable. Their confrontation with their government, from local politicians to the distant military bureaucracy, was devastating. Their salvation, of course, was each other. Families came together, sacrificed, and held on. Neighbors helped neighbors. People volunteered. Everyone learned. All around them, the angels of compassion and the demons of liability wrestled.

Later, I would contact organizations like the Pacific Studies Center and the Military Toxics Project that provided long catalogs of military environmental abuse and the damages done to public health. The Cold War, it seemed, was conducted by the militaries of the US and the Soviet Union on the environment. I met a National Public Radio reporter named Seth Shulman who interviewed me and read his book, *The Threat at Home*. It described the 20,000 toxic sites behind US military fences and the 7,000 toxic sites on foreign ground controlled by the US military, like the poisonous plume of underground water contaminated with carcinogenic solvents and paint residues that leaked from Tooele Army Depot waste lagoons and was spreading slowly towards Grantsville's wells. Dozens of extraction wells were sunk to suck up the contaminated water so it could be treated in a specially designed plant and then pumped back through dozens of injection wells to flush the plume. I thought our case was exceptional, but I learned it was typical.

I discovered how the military services routinely refused to comply with rules that were taken for granted by business, and how state and federal agencies were powerless to enforce those rules. I learned about "sacrifice zones," now well known, in Hanford, Rocky Flats, and Aberdeen. In the spring of 1993, however, I had never tangled with the military's obstinate bureaucracy. I had not been lied to. I had not experienced cover-up and incredible denial. All that would come.

Towards the end of a long weekend, I finally got some one-on-one time with an epidemiologist. He told me there was a two- to three-year waiting list for epidemiological studies because so many communities were in crisis. Generally, ATSDR did not agree to conducting a study unless it was fairly clear they were going to find a target for remediation. As he asked questions about Tooele County, it became clear that people in my community face many occupational hazards. Those that worked at the Tooele Army Depot, the major employer at the time, were exposed to solvents used to clean motors and fumes when rebuilt motors and vehicles were painted. Those that worked at the Magcorp magnesium refinery were exposed to high levels of chlorine gas and hydrochloric acid. Workers at the Kennecott copper smelter were routinely exposed to arsenic and heavy metals. Those who ranched on the side were exposed to pesticides and herbicides. Although it was depressing to consider how dangerous daily work was for friends and neighbors back home, I ended my session with the doctor feeling relieved and reassured. After all, my kids didn't work at Magcorp or the army depot, so they were probably not in harm's way.

I returned home with some powerful impressions. The citizens I met in San Diego were all politically activated by their experiences. They had paid a terrible price, knew what was at stake, and were determined to get justice and defend their health. The walking wounded I met that weekend are the new faces of the environmental movement. They carry a warning: pay attention, it could happen to you. I took the warning seriously and no longer had illusions about how dangerous it can be to live downwind or downstream from the US military.

This idea was reinforced a few weeks later when Steve Erickson of the Utah Downwinders talked me into going to Washington DC with the Sierra Club's Cindy King for a conference sponsored by the Chemical Weapons Working Group. The CWWG was an umbrella organization of community groups in chemical weapons "stockpile" sites across the nation where chemical weapons incineration was planned. According to the army's master plan for chemical weapons demilitarization, incinerators would go up in Maryland, Indiana, Kentucky, Alabama, Arkansas, Colorado, Utah, and Oregon. A prototype incinerator, the Chemical Agent Munitions Disposal System, always referred to by its acronym CAMDS, had already been burning nerve agent in Utah. A pilot, Johnston Atoll Chemical Agent Disposal System, always called JACADS, was up and burning in the Pacific. The first of the full-scale incinerators was planned for Tooele County and would be located about thirty miles southeast of my home as the crow flies, assuming it doesn't drop dead from poisonous emissions. Utah has about 40 percent of the nation's stockpile of chemical weapons, so we were scheduled to go first.

This would be the CWWG's second conference. At the first, a year earlier, representatives from the other stockpile sites thought they had a solution to the problem of how to get rid of the deadly stash of chemical weapons in their own backyards: ship it to Utah. After all, we already had the prototype incinerator and the lion's share of the nation's nerve agent. There was no way we were going to dodge the incinerator bullet. Why not limit the damage to Utah? Cindy King held her ground that year and Craig Williams from the Kentucky delegation, who was way ahead of the crowd, backed her up and threatened to keep the others from making their airline flights out if they didn't reach an agreement on accords that eliminated the transportation option. Cindy and Craig prevailed then, but the issue was likely to come up again, Erickson told me. Cindy needed someone to help her defend Utah from the transportation option.

I knew little about the issue. I was aware a lot of nerve agent was stored at the army depot's South Area, but I didn't know how much. It was not something you could come up with on your own. When I first contacted a realtor in the area to help me look for a house, I asked the usual questions. Where's the nearest school? What are the property taxes like here? I never thought to ask, "Hey, is anyone in the neighborhood sitting on a massive stash of chemical weapons?" Those shiny brochures from the Chamber of Commerce never boast about our stockpiled weapons of mass destruction.

I had watched CAMDS being constructed with the same normal innocence. The use of acronyms disguised the purpose of the project. No one said Chemical Agent Munitions Disposal System, they said "Camdus" and Camdus coulda been someone's sister for all I knew. I remember how she took shape on the horizon as I drove the bookmobile by the construction site each week on my way to a two-room schoolhouse in the pretty little village of Vernon. I remember eating lunch in the schoolhouse with one of the teachers and asking, "What is that factory going up over by the South Area?"

"An incinerator," she replied.

"What are they incinerating?" I asked.

"Nerve gas."

I laughed. "Very funny. No, really, what are they incinerating?"

"Nerve gas. Really."

Life on the rim of the West Desert was full of surprises. There were questions I had never dreamed I'd be asking and answers I was not prepared to hear. It takes a long time for the newcomer to read the litany of environmental horrors located in Tooele County because the activities that go on there can hardly be anticipated. I agreed to go to the conference with Cindy. It was another opportunity to look for clues to what was going on around me.

Transportation of chemical munitions was not seriously debated at the CWWG's '93 conference. I came prepared to debate and ended up sitting on my hands listening. Transportation was not an issue again because the citizen activists had done their homework in the intervening year. They were a varied group. There was a minister, a mechanic, a garlic farmer, a teacher, a housewife. Their numbers included some of the Cold War civilian walking wounded, especially those who lived downwind from the Hanford nuclear weapons facilities, but they were mostly sharp-witted citizens who had heard about the Department of Defense's plans and were alarmed. They understood intuitively that they could join the walking wounded if the DOD got its way.

Only one delegate, a combustion engineer, had a thorough and technical knowledge of what the army was up to and what it all meant. Everyone else had to learn about it from scratch and on their own. They had to acquire a new vocabulary, go to the library, pour through reams of government documents, and read between the lines. By '93, most understood that the stockpile was old and falling apart. A lot of it had been transported at one time, from Japan and Germany to an island in the Pacific or from Denver to Utah, but now it couldn't be moved very far. The political obstacles to transportation had become overwhelming since the wisdom of such a move would be debated and opposed from one end of any proposed road route or rail line to the other. If the army was having problems convincing eight stockpile communities to deal with nerve gas, imagine the scale of the objections that would be raised from a hundred communities along the various transportation corridors.

There was another reason transportation no longer seemed a compelling solution to containing the environmental damage from the army's "chem demil" program. The citizen activists had learned that incineration provides perverse proof of how we are all downwind and downstream from one another as our bodies incorporate our environment. Incinerators emit a well-known and dangerous category of chemicals called "dioxin" and many other chemical combinations for which there is no toxicity information at all. The members of the dioxin family are well-known bad actors and the most famous of a broader group of chemicals called "endocrine disrupters." PCBs are also well-known endocrine disrupters.

The body is a community of 50 trillion cells that must communicate to interact and live. We have three great networks that coordinate cell growth and behavior. My personal favorite is the nervous system which helps us hit fast balls and survive freeway traffic. Then there's the immune system which protects us against viruses and bacteria and is the subject of movies about Ebola outbreaks. The endocrine system, which is usually associated with acne and menopause, is not nearly as popular as the others but is also key. It controls and coordinates the body's functions through hormones in the bloodstream. Hormones are the mail carriers of the endocrine system. Estrogen and testosterone are the best known of these messengers, but more than a hundred hormones have now been identified. The hormones of the endocrine system also control fetal development.

Endocrine disruptors are pollutants that mimic hormones and, like all false messengers, sow confusion. The body's cells accept the pollutants because of their similarity to hormones. Once deep inside cells, they wreak havoc. Along with reproductive chaos and loss, endocrine disruptors have been linked to cancer, immune system toxicity, birth defects, diabetes, various chronic illnesses and even learning disorders. The Environmental Protection Agency did a major reassessment of dioxin in the mid-nineties which confirmed the damage they do. Back in the Love Canal days, dioxin was considered dangerous when we only knew it caused cancer. Now we know that cancer is just the tip of the toxic iceberg.

The evidence of how pollution becomes you now runs into

volumes. Or, if you are the kind that likes physical evidence, for about $2,000 you can get lab work done to reveal that you, like the rest of us, carry traces of about 250 synthetic industrial chemicals in your blood and tissue. The breast milk of many US mothers is so contaminated with pesticide residues and industrial chemicals that it could not be legally bottled and sold as a food commodity. Most of us are carrying loads of dioxin that are at or very close to levels the EPA believes are unsafe. When mother rats are given doses of dioxin equivalent to the amount most of us are already carrying in our bodies, their male offspring are born with tiny penises and can't reproduce. Maybe that provides a clue to why human male sperm counts have decreased 50 percent in the last fifty years while testicular cancer tripled. A typical young man today has half the sperm his granddad did. This is even true for young men who run marathons and pray daily. Dioxin and the other so-called persistent organochlorine pollutants, or POPs, are the prime suspects in derailing reproductive development in both man and beast.

Men are not alone. The dioxin family and its organochlorine cousins have also been linked to the rising number of tubal and ectopic pregnancies in women and in growing rates for breast cancer. In the Cold War era, more American women died of breast cancer than all the Americans killed in World War One, World War Two, the Korean War, and the Vietnam War combined. Since 1940, a woman's chance of getting breast cancer has doubled. The steady creeping increase in breast cancer cannot be explained by an aging population or better detection methods. In fact, less than half of breast cancers can be explained by known risk factors. A majority of the studies on the link between organochlorine pollution and breast cancer suggest a positive link. There is much other compelling evidence that breast cancer has environmental causes. Like the fact that many industrialized nations have breast cancer rates as much as five times higher than non-industrialized nations. And the daughters of women who migrate from those low-incident nations to high-incident nations acquire the breast cancer risk that prevails in their adopted high-risk homelands.

The latest research on dioxin and its chemical cousins explores the way they lower immune function so the body is vulnerable to opportunistic viruses and chronic illness. Up until recently, scientists insisted that toxins were in one conceptual box and viruses were in a separate box. That is, the two don't mix and are not related. Apples and oranges, as they say. But nature is an open and dynamic system that respects few of our conceptual boxes, no matter how useful these neat categories are to us. The way toxins and pollution contribute to chronic illness by lowering immune system function and thus opening pathways to viruses that might otherwise be resisted is a piece of the environmental/health puzzle that will soon fall into place.

The chemical weapons incinerator being built in my Utah backyard would emit dioxins. People think the danger of an incinerator is that you might be downwind from it and breathe in the bad stuff that like dioxins come out the stack. But only about 2 percent of the dioxins you will take into your body in a lifetime will be inhaled. The real danger is not to your lungs but to your dinner. About 98 percent of the dioxins we are exposed to come to us through the food we eat, especially beef and dairy products. Dioxins go out the incinerator stack, are carried by the wind, and then fall out into soil, water, plants, and animals.

From there they "bioaccumulate" up through the food chain to you and me.

Bioaccumulation means that a blade of grass may contain a tiny amount of dioxin or some herbicide or pesticide chemical. A cow, however, can eat a lot of grass. So the cow more or less gathers the dioxin or pesticide that is spread out in the pasture's grass and concentrates it in her milk, especially in the fatty cream. A dairy producer then collects the cream from many dioxin-gathering cows and further concentrates it into ice cream that you give to your daughter as a reward for winning the spelling bee. So cows gather the dioxin in the pasture and concentrate it in their cream and we gather the dioxin-laden cream in the cows and eat it. Being at the top of the food chain has its price.

Being at the top of the food chain in a global economy means that those fundamental links that make food a synthesis of water, air, and soil now stretch across the planet. The grain in your breakfast cereal may have come from a Canadian wheat field and the fruit you cut up on it may have been grown in Central America. Your coffee came from somewhere in Africa, Latin America, or Asia. The burger you ate for lunch may have been part of a steer in a Texas feedlot while the tomato slice on it may have come from California or Mexico. The beef in that burger, of course, came from a steer that was also fed grain or alfalfa from here and there in the Midwest and Great Plains. The ice cream you had for desert may have started in a Vermont dairy farm.

In fact, the origins of the food we eat are as amalgamated as the cars and appliances we buy that may have components from the US, Korea, Japan and you name it. For example, go through your pantry and read the ingredient labels on cans, boxes, and bottles. Look for corn syrup, corn gluten, cornstarch, dextrose, soy oil, or soy protein. Everything from salad dressing to soft drinks has at least one of these ingredients. Most of them come straight out of the American heartland, places like Illinois where more than 50 million pounds of pesticides are applied to crops each year. In addition, 250 million gallons of industrial waste are pumped into Illinois ground and there is evidence that waste shows up in irrigation water spread on crops. Another 100 million pounds of toxic chemicals are legally released into the Illinois environment. Each place where our food is grown has its own particular blend of pollution that finds its way into that food, but Illinois is a typical state where agriculture and industry mix. No matter where else the food we eat may have originated, if it contains corn and soy ingredients, part of it is from the Midwest and traces of chemical pollution from there are also included. We have always been linked together by dynamic atmospheric and hydrologic cycles, but it is especially through our food chain that local air, water, and soil quality issues become global concerns. My backyard is your backyard and vice versa.

So if the army builds incinerators in Alabama or Arkansas to get rid of our old and deteriorating stockpile of chemical weapons, as they are trying to do, the dioxins and other toxic chemicals emitted from burning nerve gas will fall out into the massive chicken growing operations that surround those sites. You, then, could buy a dioxin drumstick in your neighborhood food store no matter where in the country you live. For the Oregon burner being built near the Columbia River, it would be fish that are contaminated. Even in Utah, where the incinerator is out in the sagebrush and relatively isolated, a perfect distribution and delivery system is close at hand. Huge salt evaporation ponds along the south shores of the Great Salt Lake are in the fallout zone. Most of that salt is not made into table salt, but a lot of it is road salt and that goes everywhere. It is spread on roads and then runs off into streams, rivers, and groundwater, or dries up and blows away, or goes traveling on car tires and bodies.

I prefer to put this lesson more poetically by saying we are fluid creatures in a fluid world and every cell in our bodies contains the universe that flows through us without regard for the latest concepts and vocabulary we have invented to describe it. But the fact is that this profound principle of connectedness is realized in other less lyrical ways that we ignore at our peril. The CWWG delegates were quickly becoming familiar with the global game of "please pass the poison." By the time of their '93 conference they had evolved from "think locally, act locally" to "think globally, act locally."

I was changing, too. I came home with a wary eye. I began to see the Great Basin as a kind of strange attractor for all the waste of western civilization, from radioactive Cold War debris to contaminated soil from Superfund sites to the voluminous toxins that are routinely produced from our modern way of life. It had all been building up in the Great Basin for years and there was no end in sight. The more we dumped there, the more likely we would do it some more. Chemical weapons incineration was really just a second act. It had now gone on long enough to reveal an impact on public health that was dark and ominous even in denial.

Over the next two years, Lee Davidson, the Washington

correspondent for the *Deseret News*, wrote a series of articles revealing the hidden history of Dugway Proving Grounds. I started meeting former Dugway workers. I listened to the tales and testimony of colleagues at work and neighbors who had lived through atomic testing in the 1950s. I learned to speak in the acronyms of the military. I went to the library and poured through documents to assign facts to the incredible stories I was hearing. All the while I had a queasy feeling, as if what I was reading between the lines was a recipe for disaster, or perhaps a breakfast cereal recipe for two-headed babies.

SIX

COWBOYS IN GAS MASKS FIND A DAMN GOOD PLACE TO DUMP USED RAZOR BLADES

At the end of a long hot day underground, the uranium miners would walk along the ore car tracks and emerge from their dank tunnels into the open light. At the mine opening there was a Geiger counter that was swung over the surfacing ore cars to get a reading of how powerful their radioactive loads were. I once listened to a former miner from Marysvale, Utah, tell how he and his friends would turn the Geiger counter on at the end of a work day and blow on it to see who could get the highest reading from his lungs. The instrument would crackle with static as each worker exhaled hard his radioactive breath. This was done for amusement. As the only survivor of the group, he shook his head in amazement and got that thousand yard stare as he struggled to understand his own ignorance, the sad fate of his coworkers who died young of lung cancer, and his government's complicity in hiding the danger it surely knew was there. In the 1950s and 60s, he and thousands of other uranium miners, many of them poor Navajos, were expendable. The Cold War was on and we were in an arms race that required uranium quickly, too quickly for safeguards or caution. Today, among the 45,000 radioactive sites in the US that must be cleaned up, there are over 1,140 uranium mining sites in Utah. There is no count for dead miners.

The uranium ended up in bombs like those tested over the Nevada desert. Those that ran the tests waited until the wind blew towards Utah. After all, Arizona had a senator, Barry Goldwater, who was powerful and tough. You wouldn't want to piss him off by poisoning his constituents. Utah was sparsely populated with Mormons who, in the fifties, were still a small and unpopular minority, often regarded as odd outsiders within their own nation. Official documents from that time actually describe them as a "low use segment of the population." Mormons, in turn, were well aware of their status and self-conscious about their polygamist past. With their backs against the desert wall, they had built a proud society and culture that could endure hardship and they were now eager for acceptance and willing to sacrifice for inclusion. Across the globe, you can easily find non-Mormon communities plagued by the contamination from military and industrial activities. In each case you will also find that powerlessness is a key to the equation of contamination. In Utah, one classic element of powerlessness was scarcity and another was "otherness."

My friend Abel was a small boy then on his grandfather's sheep ranch. His memories of that era are few but vivid. While children in the rest of the nation were being taught to "duck'n'cover" to guard against exposure to an atomic blast, government officials and scientists actually encouraged the Utah locals who were immediately downwind from the one hundred plus nuclear blasts they conducted to go outside and watch. They could "witness a moment in history."

He remembers sitting on the roof of his family's house with his brothers and sisters. Being up on the roof was not a normal activity and they waited with the kind of anticipation children feel when sitting on a curb and waiting for a Fourth of July parade to begin. They would poke each other and tease and occasionally look up to catch a glimpse of a hawk crossing the wide desert sky. Only they were not waiting for a marching band, fire trucks, or sequined girls with batons. They were waiting for the blinding flash of a distant atomic detonation followed minutes later by a wall of hot air. It would flatten their shirts against their chests, sweep their hair back, bend the trees in the backyard, and send clouds of dust swirling. Sometimes a blizzard of hot ashes would fall later and the children would run, shout, and twirl in the summer storm of atomic debris. The ranch was remote and entertainment was where you found it.

As my friend and his siblings yelled and leaped through the radioactive dust and ashes, soldiers who had just crouched in trenches near the blast climbed from their hiding places and marched slowly towards the bruise-colored mushroom cloud in front of them. With their naked eyes, they had just studied the x-rayed bones in their hands at the moment of destruction. It was the whitest light they had ever seen. For several moments they had unwittingly become transparent glowing angels in the nuclear hell of America's Cold War jihad. Those who had defecated in their pants quickly tried to cover their shame. Soon, the soles of their boots would melt under the crunching surface of hot sand that was melted into globs of glass by the inferno. They marched right into "ground zero." Later, some vomited uncontrollably and bled from every orifice of their bodies. Days after, their hair came out when they combed it. They were young, most of them, and their lives would be short. Years later, their records were shredded and their sacrifices unacknowledged.

Abel also remembers when the family car was stopped on the way into town by government scientists who were covered from head to toe in protective suits, like spacemen. He could not see their expressions because their faces and eyes were covered with gas masks. They waved their instruments over the car tires and took notes. His father leaned out his car window and asked if all was well. No problem, the scientists told him while keeping their gas masks tight, drive on.

Then there was the "lambing shed from Hell." Rural Mormons like my friend do not use the "H word" lightly. They say "HE double toothpicks" rather than pronounce the word out loud. In heated conversations they say "my heck." In this case, however, the word Hell is said openly because it is appropriate. That spring most of the sheep that were gathered into the shed had raw patches between their wool or odd-looking bleached spots. Some had blisters around their mouths. Many aborted their fetuses and the fetuses looked like exhibits in a carnival freak show—two heads, no heads, two tails, extra legs, misshapen and hideous forms that resembled no earthly creature. Lambs that were almost as freakish followed. Some had hearts that beat outside of their chests. The normal-looking ones often sickened and died shortly after they were born.

Abel's grandfather went crazy. The sheep were his livelihood, his means of supporting his family in a desert landscape where ranching was hard and marginal. He was supposed to be the patriarch of his clan and take care of the others. To a deeply religious and simple man who did not know the ways radiation could scramble the cellular chemistry of fetal development, the events that transpired in his lambing shed that spring must have seemed a curse, some awful almighty retribution for an unknown violation.

He was not alone. The curse was widespread. As he and his neighbors traded stories, they grew suspicious, angry, and fearful. Most, however, remained silent. Like all Americans, they had experienced the collective trauma of global war, witnessed the destruction of Hiroshima and Nagasaki, and lived in fear of the Communist menace. What if Russia acquired stronger atomic weapons than we owned? They might do to us what we did to Japan. They were convinced America needed atomic weapons to defend itself and took a certain pride that the development of such weapons was happening in their own remote backyard. Mormons were well aware in those days that they were still considered odd outsiders by the rest of the nation. In the mind of America, they were closely associated with their polygamist past. They had a history of persecution. Their prophet, Joseph Smith, had been murdered and they fled across the Great Plains to the Utah desert where an army expedition was soon sent to occupy their valley and watch over them. A hundred years passed and they were still regarded warily. This was a chance to make a sacrifice and prove their patriotism. As Mormons, raised in a tight and hierarchical church that demanded obedience and loyalty, they were also inclined to accept authority and not ask questions. Step out of line and you might be shunned.

But some did question. Phone calls were made and letters written. No one wanted to hear it. Scientists were sent in to reassure the doubters. Women who complained they were losing their hair were diagnosed as "neurotic" or suffering from "housewife syndrome." Even the prominent scientist who led America's effort to develop the atomic bond, Robert Oppenheimer, was described by President Truman as a "crybaby scientist" when he tried to warn of the health risks of atmospheric nuclear testing.

Many of the ranchers went out of business. Some moved on to jobs in uranium mines and felt fortunate they could keep their heads above water. Years later, most are gone. Cancer ran rampant in those small towns that were downwind. There were respiratory, neurological, and heart diseases, too, and chronic illnesses that had no diagnosis. Economic ruin preceded the years of biopsies and tumors. My friend lost his parents and a brother in his thirties to cancer. His wife had thyroid cancer in her thirties. He has been lucky, he says, but sometimes his body feels like it is a time bomb ticking away. He reads about the genetic mutations that radiation can cause and worries that his children or grandchildren will also suffer someday.

Those who are baffled by the passivity of Utahns and their political leaders to the onslaught of military experimentation and abuse in years to come, must start with the trauma of atomic testing, the betrayal and cover-up. Denial is one way of dealing with psychic damage. Dr Robert Jay Lifton coined the phrase "nuclear numbing" to describe such behavior. Poor plus obedient plus numb plus eager to belong was a formula the military learned to use over and over to their advantage.

The story of my friend and his family and neighbors has been told. It is a story that with different circumstances but the same elements of fear, arrogance, trust, ignorance, and betrayal can be told in Hanford, Rocky Flats, Kazakhstan, or at the Nevada Test Site where more than 200 even bigger underground nuclear blasts were conducted in the years after above ground testing was banned. And lately the circle of exposure has been broadened as the secret documents continue to be discovered, released, or leaked. It wasn't just in Southern Utah that unsuspecting innocents were dosed. Clouds of radiation drifted in the wind and fell hundreds of miles away. Every community east of the prevailing winds was a player in an atmospheric game of radioactive roulette. We now know there were lots of hot spots in northern Utah, Montana, Idaho, Colorado, and South Dakota. A hard radioactive rain fell on Chicago after one test. Other fallout storms dowsed communities as far away as Troy and Rochester, New York.

Nuclear fallout reached farm-belt pastures and was passed on through milk. Children were especially vulnerable because they drink more milk and have smaller thyroids than adults. Preston Truman, an uncharacteristically indignant and tenacious downwinder, played a key role in organizing his neighbors in Southern Utah to get compensation for being in harm's way. He told me the compensation some were eventually granted was a calculated political move to head off greater and more widespread demands that politicians feared would be made as people far and wide realized that they too were dangerously exposed. Across the nation, for example, one hundred thousand cases of thyroid cancer may have been caused by the distribution of Iodine 131 from testing. That is far more than the number of cases the National Cancer Institute predicted in its "worst case scenario" just a few years ago, because each year we learn more about the extent of Iodine 131 distribution. But they ignore the impact on public health from exposure to Strontium 90, Celisium 137, Zirconium and other dangerous byproducts of atomic testing that were also released into the wind. There could be hundreds of thousands of uncalculated cancers, to say nothing of the heart disease, neurological disorders, chronic illnesses, birth defects, and sterility that were certainly fueled by radiation.

Farther north, at the Dugway Proving Grounds in Utah, the sons of poor farmers ran to their places on a grid that was laid out along the sagebrush flat by military scientists. They were shirtless under the hot desert sun but that was necessary. When the scientists released the mosquitoes, the men were told to stand still and wait to be bitten. The bites would be recorded and then injections given. The mosquitoes were carrying encephalitis.

Memories of the Great Depression were powerful and the men were thankful they had secure employment with the government. "It's good work if you can get it," they told each other. Hazard pay was an extra 6 cents an hour or 48 cents a day. They were sure the shots the docs gave them would work and they were proud to be part of something so much bigger than they were. It appealed to their homegrown patriotism. They were defending the free world. When they were mindful of the risk they were taking, they justified it by thinking of the soldier in some future battle whose life they might be saving. The carnage and trauma of World War Two was still fresh in their minds.

Dugway was busy. Other workers were setting out cages of rabbits in the salt flats. When the animals were set, shells containing nerve agent were fired into the grid where they burst and set loose clouds of nerve gas around the startled animals.

Cameras whirred as the rabbits' eyes watered. Seconds later they would twitch violently and then go rigid as the nerve agent paralyzed their muscles so they could not take a breath. They suffocated and died. Take out a quarter, a former Dugway worker told me, and look at George Washington's eye. "If you covered his eye with nerve agent," he said, "you'd have yourself a lethal dose."

Rabbits died weekly from 1959 to 1969 to impress soldiers attending chemical warfare orientation sessions conducted at Dugway then. The soldiers would watch over closed-circuit television to understand the power of chemical warfare agents. Eventually the show became more varied as guinea pigs, dogs, horses, cows, monkeys, and even antelope were added to the mix of demonstration targets. After each show, civilian employees walked into the target areas, still contaminated with gas, and collected the bodies and transported them to the base lab. They wore no protective clothing. A few had gas masks because they broke into a locked supply room and stole them. Those who were too afraid to steal went into the site with bare lungs. Years later, protective clothing was used but it was primitive and, on summer days, unbearably hot. Often, they would yank off gas masks and rubber suits as soon as they were out of the immediate target area, unmindful of the danger from the contaminated suits and gear that they dropped beside them.

Although the brains of our chemical warfare program remained for the most part in Fort Detrick, Maryland, Dugway was where the action was. An expanse of Great Basin high desert the size of Rhode Island, Dugway's sage flats, salt flats, and stony rolling hills were ideal for experimenting with munitions filled with nerve agent. In the wake of the big war, a staff was recruited and planted in the isolated dry zone that had been designated for sacrifice. The work was grim, of course, not your inspirational equivalent of finding a cure for cancer, and the living conditions were crude, cloistered, and intellectually claustrophobic. Only misfits and derelicts tend to tolerate such circumstances, and Dugway's scientific community evolved into a strange breed indeed. A survivor of that era claims experimental results were often "dry-labbed," meaning they were manipulated when data did not match desires. How they could justify violations to the empirical creed of their profession and the risks others were taking to carry out their experiments is hard to discern. Maybe it was a classic case of the ends justifying the means. Maybe they believed those others were expendable. Maybe they were just reckless. Maybe their own grandiose faith in technological prowess blinded them to the consequences of their endeavors. Maybe Cold War anticommunist hysteria affected them. How about "all of the above"? Whatever their motives, their behavior over the history of Dugway Proving Grounds displayed the characteristics you'd expect from a bunch of traumatized, addicted, amnesiacs.

The biggest challenge in using chemical weapons is controlling the kill zone. Chemical munitions were originally designed as strategic weapons. Say your enemy is racing your troops towards an important junction or strategic position and they get ahead of you. You fire your chemical munitions into the junction to make your enemy wait for the gas to disperse so you can catch up. Of course, that's not the way it worked in World War One. Fired at close range to kill troops, mustard gas sometimes blew back on the army using it or drifted out of the target area, killing adjacent allied soldiers. Nerve agent, the army realized, would be even harder to control and every kind of ammunition they had packed with it would disperse it differently. Between 1951 and 1969 there were 1,635 field trials. More than 55,000 chemical rockets, artillery shells, bombs, and land mines were blown up to understand how they could be used. Airplanes flew over test grids and sprayed nerve agent to see how it was dispersed in various weather conditions and at various heights. All totaled, a half million pounds of nerve agent was released into the open wind. That's the equivalent of 3.5 trillion lethal doses.

Of course, targets were often missed and sometimes the ammunition didn't explode. When it could be found, Dugway workers dug it up. Imagine, one of them told me, digging in the mud for an unexploded rocket filled with nerve gas. It's very quiet, he said, because everyone is listening for the sound of that first shovel hitting metal. They couldn't find it all. Unexploded ordinance covers thousands of acres of the base. Now referred to as "non-stockpile chemical munitions," these deadly misfires must be cleaned up and destroyed. It will cost taxpayers billions.

The army didn't even contain its tests and training to its own ground. A Department of the Interior study shows about 1,400 square miles of public land in Utah is covered with unexploded ordinance, some of it containing nerve agent and germs. When walking or riding on BLM land adjacent to military property, it is wise to stick to the road in front of you. You never know where the chemical ghosts of the Cold War may be lurking.

Despite all the testing and practice, they never had much success putting the nerve gas on the target. On 13 September

1962, for example, they test dropped 2,800 pounds of VX agent but only 4 percent reached the target grid. The other 96 percent of that load was sown into the wind. "Recovery rates" of 10 to 30 percent were common. Dispersing agent from high altitudes or great distances proved most difficult and high winds were another complicating factor. No one knew where all that nerve gas went that missed the grids, but then no one was looking for it either.

The weather was far from optimal on 13 March 1968. There were ominous thunderheads building and shifting winds. It was not the best day to play with nerve gas, but a bunch of VIPs were visiting and they wanted to see some action. The Dugway crew was eager to show off. The test was named "Operation Combat Kid." A Phantom fighter jet loaded with more than a ton of nerve agent in a spray tank closed in on its target and expelled its load. And then some. Apparently a valve didn't close and about twenty pounds of the VX agent the plane was carrying was inadvertently sprayed well beyond the target zone. It may have been sucked into a storm cell then rained out downwind. One way or the other it ended up in Skull Valley, almost thirty miles away. At first, birds and rabbits died. Sheep followed. Over the next two days, 6,400 would perish. One by one, they sickened, dropped, shuddered, and expired.

The army quarantined the crew of the Phantom for several weeks to keep them from talking and scoffed at the notion that the sheep died from nerve agent. Only minuscule traces were found on grass. Sheep, of course, can eat a lot of grass. They keep their noses to the ground and breathe in whatever is there. Eventually, the soldiers collected the carcasses and buried them. Today, they can't remember where. An archaeologist has been hired to locate the mass graves. The government eventually paid out a million dollars in compensation while denying responsibility.

The sheep kill got national attention. Soon after, Nixon banned open-air testing of nerve gas. Even so, some agent testing continued. Mostly, however, the army switched to various chemical simulants and kept at it until the 1980s. Although safer than nerve gas, the health hazards of the simulants has also been questioned. At least some are carcinogenic.

The army never admitted they killed the sheep. They certainly never took responsibility for Ray Peck. Peck and his family were living and working on a rented ranch in Skull Valley then. During Operation Combat Kid, Ray was clearing a ditch with a tractor between two sheep herds that died. Ray remembers the following morning as being crisp and clear. There was nothing atypical about it except for some dead birds on the ground and a rabbit dying in the distance he noticed on his way to do his chores. The helicopter that later landed in his backyard, however, was unusual. It carried army officials who wanted to collect the dead wildlife and conduct blood tests on him and his frightened family. The other Skull Valley ranch families, sheepherders, and Goshute Indians who could be located were also rounded up and tested.

The tests measured levels of cholenesterase, an enzyme needed for nerves to send messages. The army scientists assured the Peck family and the others that they showed normal results, though the results were inconclusive. They had no cholenesterase baseline for the family or its community and no follow up was done. In fact, the army did less testing on the human beings in that valley than on the sheep—but their liability for the sheep might be contested and they were eager for any data on sheep they could work into their case for denial. The local people, as they had been learning, would believe experts, would not challenge army brass, and were reluctant to bite the hand that fed them. Everyone in the valley had a neighbor or relative who was employed at Dugway. Even independent ranchers might work part time there. It could be safely assumed the locals would give up and fade away. And they did.

Twenty-five years later, however, *Deseret News* reporter Lee Davidson located Ray Peck. Peck told Davidson that in the days after the '68 sheep kill the entire family came down with diarrhea and had earaches and trouble breathing. Army docs told them they had the flu, an unfortunate coincidence. From 1968 on, the Peck family suffered violent and debilitating headaches. They had not suffered headaches before then. Ray had strange numbness and burning sensations in his leg. Worse, he had bouts of paranoia and became so terrified of making a mistake at work that he would become immobilized. He lost two jobs that way. Although there was no family history of reproductive problems before that spring day, afterwards Mrs Peck had two stillbirths and the Peck daughters had several miscarriages.

The story of the Peck family suggests that even minuscule exposure to nerve agent can be damaging, but it is what army lawyers, their contractors, and state regulators call "anecdotal" evidence. It doesn't count. Because the authorities did not follow up, there is no data. No data, no deal. Ray Peck and company are on their own. As Ray discovered, if you are going to be a victim of military testing, your chances of getting justice are best if there are lots of other victims you can contact and organize. If you are alone or in small numbers, or if a lot of time has passed and your fellow victims have moved away, the responsible powers will roll right over you.

When they weren't busy setting out live animals and monitors for nerve gas testing, and then collecting dead animals and data afterwards, the Dugway workers also helped conduct biological warfare testing. Same problem as nerve gas. How do you control it? Probably the first recorded instance of germ warfare took place in 1346 when Tartar warriors catapulted plague-ridden corpses over the walls of the besieged city of Kaffa to infect their enemies within it. But what if you used a jet plane with an aerosol mixture of germs? What about explosive munitions? Would the germs survive the blast? What if the wind was blowing? At least 328 open air experiments were conducted to find out. Anthrax, Q fever, parrot fever, rabbit fever, undulant fever, valley fever and other pathogens were used.

During some of those tests the wind was blowing hard — 30 to 60 miles per hour. In such cases, it was hard to land the germs on the test grid. Sometimes, no germs at all could be found on the test grids and it was assumed the germs had missed the target. But it was hard to know. As one test report stated, anthrax spores could not be found on four of the test plots "due in part to a heavy windstorm that cut into these plots and blew away surface soil and organisms." What eluded them first, the germs or common sense?

Landing germs on the targets was also problematic when height and speed were factors. Although the army assured Congress that strict meteorological controls were always in place, in one test, bombs filled with undulant fever and other pathogens the army will not disclose were dropped out of a plane at 25,000 feet and detonated at 10,000 feet. Guess where the germs went. They did.

In another test in 1958, 40 gallons of a Q fever slurry was sprayed from an F-100A jet traveling just under the speed of sound. A single organism of Q fever can initiate a deadly infection and billions of organisms can be present in a mere drop of slurry. The army told the public there was no evidence that significant amounts of the germs they used ever migrated off base. But one report shows that although no Q fever was detected in local wildlife before it was introduced through Dugway, it had reached epidemic proportions in wildlife by 1960. It was decided to continue testing with Q fever because by that time further testing would do no harm. Other internal documents indicated a concern by army officials that the deadly and disfiguring anthrax spores they were using were showing up by Route 40, now Interstate 80. In fact, one test cloud apparently passed over the highway at an altitude of more than a mile. The local sheriff was quietly asked to record the license plate numbers of motorists who passed over the highway on test days. What happened to those numbers and the drivers who belonged to them is not known.

The disregard for the health and wellbeing of citizens was not limited to the Utah locals. Pathogens were also released in San Francisco, Washington DC, and other cities to track their dissemination in unwitting hosts. Gerald Vowles, who supervised testing at Dugway, also conducted pathogen testing using the New York City subway system. The germs they distributed there were supposedly benign but they did make people sick. That was the point. And they could be fatal to the elderly and babies. Former Dugway employee Michael Outzen claims he participated in secret testing done in Hawaii and Panama. Both men believed at the time that what they were doing was right and safe. When challenged about the risks to the public from their activities, such individuals are quick to point out that their own families live in the vicinity and they would never consider endangering them. Vowles is now in a wheelchair when he can make it out of bed. Outzen had a heart attack at age thirty-one and arthritis at thirty-seven. They see it differently now.

Most of the testing, however, was done with consent, though it would be hard to say "informed" consent. Most of the human guinea pigs probably did not understand the experimental nature of the shots they were given to guard them or the cumulative impact of injections on their immune systems. They had complete faith in the army and the miracle of medicine. A record of a test in which a cloud generator pushed Q fever towards sixty-four monitoring stations also lists seventy-five rhesus monkeys and thirty soldiers as participants. The soldiers were then flown to Fort Detrick, Maryland, for observation. There were no immediate fatalities, but the health history of the test subjects after they were discharged is not known.

In a 1977 report to Congress on eighteen years of biological warfare testing, the army claimed every possible precaution had been taken to be sure its workers, public health, and the environment were safeguarded and they could find no evidence of adverse effects. Eleven years later Congress held more hearings on the biological warfare or "BW" program while considering a new test lab for Dugway and the possibility of renewed "aerosol" testing. By then, it was clear the army had lied in the earlier reports. But that was water under the bridge, apparently.

The army, as usual, claimed it had tightened up and announced a new effort to eradicate potential dangers. Only simulants were used now, they said, and Congress signed off on them again.

Simulants were used for years after the Skull Valley sheep kill and widely accepted as safe by the guardians of official science. Who could doubt they were less risky than the real thing? With safety endorsements in hand, the military used "harmless" bacteria and simulants on targets in Hawaii, Alaska, St Louis, Minneapolis, Key West, and many other cities. The history of simulant use at Dugway over forty-five years, however, shows that time and time again they have stopped using simulants because they discovered they could be deadly. Their discoveries were always belated, long after evidence had surfaced in the medical literature. For example, zinc cadmium sulfide was used for years after it was listed as a carcinogen.

By the 1980s, Dugway wanted a "BL-4 lab" for experimenting with anthrax, bubonic plague, botulism, and deadly new strains of viruses that had their DNA tweaked for maximum lethality and resistance to known cures. They proclaimed their need for aerosol testing, too. To their surprise and chagrin, the people of Utah did not roll over as expected. By then, Preston Truman, the tenacious survivor of atomic testing from Hurricane, Utah, who had founded Downwinders Inc., had a hard earned distrust of military assurances. Truman grew up with kids who were dying of leukemia and he had buried his mother when she died of cancer. Truman and his right-hand man and consummate activist, Steve Erickson, were organizing other survivors to get compensation from the US government. When Dugway's plans for a death lab surfaced, they turned their attention hard on the new threat to public health and safety. The Utah Medical Association, local ranchers, and college students were enlisted to oppose the lab. The near total inability of Utah's medical facilities to handle an outbreak was underlined. The lab was stalled again and again. Every time it was beaten back, military planners would rally, readjust the lab's mission, and march their disguised death lab down the corridors of power yet again. Along the way, questions were raised about untested vaccines given to Gulf War troops and whether they were being used as unwitting guinea pigs in a dry run at chemical/biological warfare defense, and about the sale of biological materials by the US to the Iraq's Atomic Energy Commission before the war.

By 1998, the Pentagon finally found a costume that could get its little monster through the door and a new lab was finally built, though well below the Apocalyptic expectations of Dugway's fevered crew. The drumbeat for increased testing at Dugway has become louder as we are warned of the dangers of biological weapons in the hands of terrorists or Saddam Hussein. There is a proposal to build a full-scale town at Dugway that could be used for chemical and germ warfare training. The military wants better protective gear, detectors, and vaccines. This would all be "defensive," of course. But you cannot design an effective defense without imagining and simulating the offense you are defending against. Even those in the military who want bigger chemical and biological warfare budgets cannot say where the line between offense and defense is drawn. It is a two-sided coin. So far, the only American casualties of biological and chemical warfare have been citizens harmed by the very military sworn to defend them and Gulf

War troops who put each other in harm's way when they blew up Saddam's stash.

Not to be outdone by those boys over at the Nevada Test Site, Dugway's Cold War cowboys also conducted radiation dispersal tests, about seventy that we know. The really big stuff was being detonated at the south end of the desert, so Dugway was left with testing little ammo, like radioactive dust grenades and 1,000 pound cluster bombs.

Some of the tests defy explanation. In 1959, mock-ups of eight small nuclear reactors were intentionally melted down. Sensors were set up over a 210 square mile area. They indicated that in one test alone about fourteen times more curies of radiation was released than in the infamous Three Mile Island nuclear reactor accident.

Why did they do it? A proposal had been made to design a plane that would be fueled by a small nuclear reactor. Impossible, critics said, reactors are too heavy and such a plane could not get off the ground. Although a consensus quickly formed around the case against the plane and it was clear it would never get off the drawing board, the army still wanted to find out what would happen if the mythical beast crashed and burned. So they melted reactor fuel in furnaces to simulate eight meltdowns. In all, the curies released from radiation testing at Dugway were 10,000 times those released at Three Mile Island.

Even when workers were not voluntarily exposed, the exposure of Dugway workers seemed to be inevitable. Aside from working in an environment where nerve gas, pathogens, and radiation were always drifting about or contaminating the dust that blew in their faces and the ground they walked on, workers were constantly handling contaminated equipment. Protective clothing and ways to decontaminate equipment were tested. Workers collected the contaminated gear and washed down contaminated equipment with solutions that were themselves carcinogenic. Most accepted that exposure was part of the job and counted on the shots to protect them.

Anyone familiar with army construction projects or maneuvers knows that the "oops factor" can be considerable. Once, they contaminated their own runway when a secret pathogen was spilled. At Dugway, the combination of so many farm and blue-collar backgrounds mixed in with unfamiliar and sophisticated field laboratory processes, unseen pathogens, and powerful chemicals made for lots of mishaps and exposures. At least one may have been deadly. Gerald Vowles still chokes up when he talks about the friends he lost when a helicopter went down over Dugway. "I just know nerve gas got loose in there."

Today, many of Dugway's former employees are ill. Too many, says Bev White. She has a list of 300 men who worked there who are now suffering cancer, multiple sclerosis, arthritis, and strange debilitating symptoms. A survey done in 1995 of 177 former workers showed fifty-five had cancer, fifty-two had heart disease, and eighteen, a whopping 10 percent, had multiple sclerosis. Vowles is confined to a wheelchair because of MS. He suspects his illness is work related because he knows he was exposed at least ten times to biological or chemical warfare agents. He got lots of experimental shots, too. Some were the same shots Gulf War vets suspect may have made them ill upon their return.

Most of the members of the Dugway League, organized by

White to ask for compensation to help defray steep medical costs, cannot get their medical records. Some records were not kept, others were lost, and some destroyed when a warehouse in St Louis burned. Vowles got his records, but the years 1955 to 1972 are missing. Another worker discovered that his records disappeared from his private doctor's office. White, a former state legislator, is appalled at how requests for medical records are met with excuses, denial, and obfuscation. Most of the men she has tried to help have been ill and ailing since they were in their thirties and forties. They are not, she insists, merely suffering the ravages of old age. They are proud individuals who are not inclined to complain. They trusted their government and now their government has abandoned them, ignoring their clear need for help and waiting, she fears, for them either to grow too weak to pursue their grievances or just to die off. The army has refused to do a follow-up study on the health of these men. Like the uranium miners, the atomic soldiers, and the downwinders, they are the unacknowledged casualties of the Cold War battles conducted in the deserts of the West.

Workers may not have been the only ones to suffer. It is unreasonable to think that fallout from nerve agent, germ, and radiation testing has had no impact on the health of those civilians who lived downwind. Over the winter of 1995–96, I organized about three dozen neighbors and we conducted a health survey of our community that confirmed our suspicion that the cellular chemistry and genetic memories of Rush Valley natives, like my Grantsville neighbors, were scrambled, scratched, and dented during Cold War testing on the West Desert.

We never used those weapons in warfare. No foreign soldiers, only our own people were exposed. The danger and risk continue long after the era of reckless testing. Today thousands of bombs, rockets, shells, land mines, and half-ton containers are scattered across the desert landscape. While attention has focused on the chemical munitions stored in hundreds of reinforced bunkers in eight stockpiles from one end of the country to the other and how to get rid of them, these "non-stockpile" munitions must also be treated. The expense cannot be realistically calculated at this time, but it will be astronomical.

Skull Valley is quiet now. No one is exactly sure where all those dead sheep are buried. Their graves are unmarked, like those of the lepers who had been converted by the Mormons in Hawaii and brought over to "Zion" before their symptoms showed. They were quarantined to Skull Valley in the nineteenth century to live out their lives in dusty isolation. The desert is for exiles. As in 1968, only a handful of ranches hang on now, most owned by distant corporations that need tax write-offs and run by hired hands. A small band of Goshute Indians live on a reservation in the middle of the valley. Eastern and Midwestern utilities have offered to make each member a millionaire if they will agree to park spent nuclear fuel rods on their land. The band's leadership has decided to take the money and run. They've purchased expensive new suits and go to meetings with highly paid lawyers. After watching from afar for so long, they now have a chance to win big in the great American economic sweepstakes. Some, however, have no price. Margene Bullcreek is leading a small group of "traditionals" who do not want their ancestral ground contaminated with civilization's most poisonous waste. "Mother Earth is not for sale," she declares. The venal dealings of the Skull Valley Goshutes is disorienting to those who associate Native Americans with more holistic and reverent environmental philosophies. But the Goshutes have been broken by alcoholism, suicide, and poverty. They have been shoved aside and ignored for too long and now they want a piece of the action.

They did not have to look far to figure out where to cut a deal. In the 1980s Tooele County commissioners created a huge hazardous waste zone in the West Desert, just beyond Skull Valley and the reaches of the Dugway Proving Grounds. Today, two commercial hazardous waste incinerators, a hazardous waste landfill, and a radioactive materials landfill sit in that zone and generate handsome revenues. They form a kind of complementary infrastructure. But there is no need to get conspirational to explain the existence of so many highly toxic enterprises on the desert floor. We have always used deserts that way. At the time of the first atomic testing, an armed forces magazine described the high desert plains of Nevada and Utah as "a damn good place to dump used razor blades."

That attitude still prevails. More than a dozen proposals to expand military training ranges in Arizona, California, Colorado, Idaho, Nevada, New Mexico, and Utah are alive and well. Although each proposed expansion is pursued separately, they add up to one big Western American training range, an empire of millions of acres of bombing ranges, electronic target zones, airfields, radar facilities, and restricted air space. Groups like the Rural Alliance for Military Accountability, directed by Grace Potori, struggle to expose the deals and impacts, but it is an uphill battle. State and local political leaders almost always support home-state military bases because they provide jobs and economic activity that are especially hard to come by in rural desert areas.

Deserts are the carpet civilization sweeps its trash under. The military testing and bombing ranges were just a door opener. The military's desert kingdom set the pattern for the corporate colonizers who followed. Given our profound alienation from the West's less colorful and appealing deserts, it was a pattern that was easy to anticipate. The logical jump for a culture that is willing to load redrock canyons with cows and conduct a predator holocaust to killing antelope with nerve gas is an easy one to make. The proposal to turn the Great Basin into a nuclear missile theme park is less surprising when you know that peculiar history of land use. By the time we got around to incinerating hazardous waste and chemical weapons in the desert air shed, the pattern was more like a well-worn groove. Parking spent fuel rods that will be radioactive for 10,000 years on the desert floor is just the next step. A congressional candidate once told me that Utah's vast barren desert was an unappreciated economic asset. Everything we make, he said enthusiastically, involves some kind of toxic byproduct that has to be disposed. "You people who live out here have something everyone else needs—a place to bury their waste."

Although it is already hard to remember, we once thought of the oceans that way and it wasn't long ago. I remember as a boy visiting the New Jersey coast and watching barges loaded with garbage and sewage sludge heading out to sea. Clouds of squawking seagulls followed their wake. My dad got hepatitis and almost died from eating oysters contaminated with sewage. The first program to get rid of aging chemical weapons was labeled CHASE, an acronym for "cut holes and sink 'em." The munitions filled with mustard and nerve gas were loaded on to old navy ships that were towed out to sea. Once they were far from land, holes were cut in the sides of the ships and they sunk with their toxic cargoes to the ocean floor.

Today we shake our heads in wonder that we could have ever been so ignorant and reckless. We understand that we cannot poison the oceans without risking grievous harm to our own landlocked wellbeing. We have not learned that lesson when it comes to our deserts. We act as if they are exempt from the dynamics of nature. As if the wind does not blow across their surfaces, carrying dust and churning what we have buried there. As if waters do not flow underneath them. As if what is out of sight does not exist. As if the collective decisions we make about what we allow into our air, water, and soil, even in deserts, are not eventually translated into someone's flesh and blood and living daily experience.

Deserts are hard to defend because their local populations are often small, scattered, and desperate for economic advantage. They are no match for big government and its corporate allies with clever lawyers, fat public relations budgets, and professional lobbyists. Because the terms and criteria of our public debates over how land is used are "practical" or utilitarian, it is hard to protect ground that offers no obvious other economic benefit. Because politicians, policy makers, and the public are not ecologically literate, the connections between what happens in the "barren wastelands" and what shows up in the blood and cells of those who live downwind are also hard to convey.

Those of us who love deserts appreciate their spare qualities. Deserts are where the rhythms and patterns of nature are written on open landscapes beneath open skies. Uplifted layers of rock like the Book Cliffs in southeastern Utah are so called because their history of deposition can be read like the pages of a book. Meandering patterns of green spell out where nourishing water spills and spreads so that patterns of elevation are shadowed by patterns of vegetation. Dark evergreens mark shadowed north faces where snow accumulates and melts slowly, while shrubs that demand less moisture than trees but more than grass and brush form the penumbras. Wind deposits dunes in graceful undulating layers topped with soft ripples. The desert is a canvass where wind, water, geological powers and the biosphere paint overlaying patinas that reveal the close interplay and relation of one to the other.

Deserts scar easily, so they are also a medium for man to carve a portrait of his activities and the fears and misunderstandings that motivate them. Stand at the top of Deseret Peak in the Stansbury Mountains and face northeast and you can see row upon row of fortified bunkers spreading out like so many rivets across the desert floor. Beige cuts announce security roads along the perimeters and fence lines. Open detonation pits pock the eastern valley. Look to the west by Grassy Knolls and you can see the faint traces of giant hazardous waste cells in the distance. On a clear day you might catch the exclamation of an incinerator smokestack.

The history of the Cold War is also written into the sand and soil, but it is harder to read. You need sophisticated instruments to read the persistent fallout that can still be detected and measured in the attic dust of our homes. Although signs and fences mark the no man's land where biological warfare tests were done, it takes a lab to find the tiny spores of anthrax mixed into the soil. There is no measure for the fear, mistrust, and hatred that put them there.

Ultimately, it is our fate we are describing on the desert landscape. Cowboys in gas masks have dumped too many used razor blades in my backyard. The time has come to write new patterns there. It is time to heal the wounded and clear the air.

SEVEN

HOW TO ORGANIZE BOILING FROGS

Have you ever thought about how much we resemble boiling frogs? I don't mean physically, though once in a locker room at a hot spring I saw a guy who came darn close. I am referring to the boiling frog analogy.

I first heard the analogy years ago in conversation on a rough bank of the Green River. We were going down Desolation Canyon on rafts and we had stopped for lunch in the shade of a generous old cottonwood. River trips are healing experiences and the perspectives of their participants shift as balance is restored. Those who are rattled unwind and those who are preoccupied and distracted let go, breathe deep, and focus anew. By the end of the trip, philosophical observations are common and natural. I can't remember who used the boiling frog analogy in conversation that hot afternoon, but I remembered it and I was impressed. I thought it was original. Years later I read the analogy in Daniel Quinn's *The Story of B*. Then I came across an earlier version attributed to Sonia Johnson.

Johnson's story goes like this. A biology teacher brings two frogs to class. He gently lowers one frog into a pan of water that he sets on a hotplate. He increases the heat under the pan gradually so that the water temperature rises slowly and the frog adjusts to it little by little. The water temperature and the frog's tolerance rise together until the frog is floating placidly in a torpid stupor. Finally, at long last, the water breaks into a boil and the frog dies before the eyes of the horrified students. Then the teacher removes the dead frog and retrieves the second frog. He drops the fresh frog into the boiling pan and it immediately reacts and leaps out.

The point, the teacher tells his students, is that we, like the first frog, survive day in and day out by adjusting down. Little by little, rainforests burn, our soil and food are poisoned, wetlands are paved over while traffic increases, cancer spreads, species die, and the temperature of the planet is literally rising. We accept, adjust, rationalize, and deny. We call it progress, call it normal, call it inevitable. When the fear arises that what is happening around us and to us is dangerous and wrong, we suppress it and look away. After all, our fellow frogs are not alarmed and acting up, so why should we? We conform and carry on. Be a smart frog, the teacher says at the end of the story, and don't adjust. Jump!

Quinn's version of the analogy appears as a fictional lecture by the mythical and mysterious leader named "B" in *The Story of B*. B uses the boiling frog analogy to trace the history of our culture from its beginnings thousands of years ago in "totalitarian agriculture" through the development of cities, kingdoms, nations, contemporary religions, and global industrialism. As Quinn tells it, the story of civilization and its "progress" is accompanied by ever-more alienation, illness, and violence, culminating in the brutal world wars and genocides of the modern era. His broad sweep is intended to remind us that the ecocrises we face today have very deep roots and that we, too, have become dazed and immobilized slowly, almost imperceptibly, to the dysfunction and degradation around us that we pass off as "normal."

Almost everyone I know who has encountered the boiling frog story relates to it easily. All of us can cite an example of someone falling into debt, a marriage or career unraveling, or some other situation where the slow accretion of events blinds the hapless victim until it is too late. Beyond personal situations, the analogy speaks to our collective modern circumstances. But although it illustrates how we tolerate the intolerable and are numbed to peril, it says little about what we can do to become smart frogs.

From 1992, when I heard stories about illness and death in my community, until 1995, I struggled to get myself out of the boiling pan I was in. I had created a comfortable and nurturing way of life for myself during the first fifteen years I lived in Grantsville. I had a modest career as a librarian that I found meaningful and rewarding even though the pay and prestige were low. Linda had likewise gained confidence and stature as a teacher. My oldest son, Brian, left for college and I had two teenagers at home, Carly and Tyler. The teenage years were good to us and our home was still the warm nest we had carefully woven years before. We had friends to enjoy and beautiful destinations to hike and climb with them. Life was good. It was certainly worth defending. But every comfort and blessing was also a reason to stay put and shelter inward. If it ain't broke, after all, why fix it? Who needs new risks and commitments that might be troublesome and upsetting? For a long time, I just hoped someone would come along and do something about the upsetting information and questions I was encountering, but by the autumn of 1995, I was ready to jump. For me, it was a process of elimination until all my emotional escape routes closed.

Political action begins with compelling awareness. That is, we become aware of an issue, a threat, a problem, a need, or an opportunity that grabs our attention in a powerful way. I have learned that once that happens, I will have to do something. Once I am aware, doing nothing is no longer an option, although I can pretend it is and fail to recognize the mental and emotional acrobatics I will go through to maintain my failure to act. Over time, I have become so familiar with these psychogyrations that I am convinced, in the end, it is simply easier to act.

I correct myself. There is denial. Denial is like a short circuit of compelling awareness. One becomes aware of a problem to the extent that it is perceived as a threat. At that point, denial kicks in like the cavalry of forgetfulness riding to the rescue. We're all familiar with the situation. For example, take the parents whose child is heavily involved with alcohol or drugs. All the signs are right under their nose but they refuse to see. If they don't see, they don't have to deal with it, and dealing with it can be difficult, upsetting, and messy. So let's just look the other way until Johnny goes into a coma.

Many people today are in a similar state of denial when it comes to the state of their environment. Auto-immune illnesses from Aids to asthma are increasing dramatically, cancer rages on, sperm counts are down, species are dying off in droves, and it's getting to the point where ordinary sunlight is dangerous, but, hey, what problem? Just slap on some more sunscreen and turn up the radio. To me, denial is not only dangerous, since it blinds me to remediating action until it may be too late, it is also the worst kind of dishonesty. It is self-deception. It walls me off from my own power to see, to act, to succeed.

But suppose one becomes aware and does not slip into denial. What then? If I choose not to act, what are my other choices? What kinds of mental gymnastics will I have to perform in order to remain inactive?

Well, there's always guilt. You know you should or could do something but you don't. Then you feel bad. Personally, I find guilt so burdensome and draining that I can't imagine any proactive or responsible behavior that is more effort and trouble. I'll choose being tired, frustrated, and overcommitted to guilt any day.

We can rationalize. "I could do something if … I would do something but …" How often have you heard excuses, elaborate excuses, when even a little effort could make a difference? Rationalization is a lot of work and requires constant maintenance, since you must talk yourself and the world around you into whatever rationalization you're making. It, too, is dishonest and self-deceptive. It is also very unsatisfying. It's so hard to feel good about yourself when you are frequently required to whine.

Distraction is the primary means of disengagement in our culture today. We have made an art of distraction. Faced with a problem you find threatening and wish to ignore? Get drunk, get laid, get lost in the game on TV, go shopping, or eat. Play Nintendo. Distraction, unlike guilt and rationalization, can actually be fun. Unfortunately, it is also self-defeating. Even Nero had to put down his fiddle and look up when the flames got too high and too close.

So what? Who cares? It doesn't matter. You can't win.

Cynicism is another way we can deal with troubling awareness. I have toyed with cynicism and found that, given the evidence of violence, stupidity, and greed in the world today, it was easy. Slipping into cynicism is as easy as giving into temptation. Cynicism is, in fact, encouraged. The polluters and degraders of our environment and those who defend them count on public cynicism to help them get their way. Every self-serving politician and bureaucrat, corporate shark, or slick PR operative who ever decided to pull one over on us, rob us, cheat us, and get away while we're not looking, used our cynicism to their advantage. They want us to stay dumb, keep quiet, look away, and settle for less. To be cynical, then, is to be a sucker, to contribute to your own undoing. Worse, it is a form of spiritual suicide, a slow cancerous death of the soul. Not recommended. Don't try this at home.

Aside from the psychological cost of "doing nothing," failure to act may also have a steep price in tangible results. When your environment is at stake, those results may include fouled air and water, contaminated soil and food, a reduced quality of life, sickness, and even death. Such negative impacts are, ultimately, the bottom line in any argument for doing something versus doing nothing. Regret may also be a consequence for those who do nothing.

Given such unattractive options, one could make a powerful case that acting on one's concerns, as difficult as that may be, is simply easier than "doing nothing." Taking action allows me to live my life unlimited by denial, unburdened by guilt, and without excuses. I can look at life directly, without the need for distraction. Pessimism is easy when I stand off to the side and watch. Optimism grows from action and engagement.

However, action should not be taken just because it is the path of least resistance, or even because it is the right thing to do, but because taking action is a wise and satisfying choice. Getting smart, reaching out, standing up, and speaking out is personally and profoundly empowering. To act is to gain valuable experiences, to acquire skills and understandings, and to build relationships with interesting people. If you become politically active you will no doubt experience frustration and defeat sometimes, but you will also win sometimes, and winning is very rewarding.

When I returned from San Diego in the spring of 1993 I tried to reassure Linda that illness in Grantsville was occupational in origin and our kids were safe, but the worries persisted. She was teaching at the local elementary school and became aware of how many children in town were suffering from birth defects. We realized that from our front porch we could point to three houses where children were in wheelchairs, one where a child had a shunt, and another where a child was missing a kidney. We could also point to two homes where kids had died of cancer. And there were so many stories. One woman in town buried her mother who was in her early fifties in the spring and her toddler daughter in the fall. What was going on that afflicted and killed children?

We wondered if we should move, but where? At the San Diego conference, I met people from Alaska who were defending their community's health from military pollution in those far corners of our nation. There seemed to be nowhere to run and, besides, we knew better. One way or another, it is all connected. The year after Chernobyl blew in the Soviet Union, songbirds died in North America. Into what corner of this world has the troubled hand of our modern Mammon not reached? Each place has its individual history and configuration of environmental hazards, some more dire than others, but the notion of a safe locale is an illusion. No, we decided to make a stand where we were.

For more than a year, we wrote letters and made phone calls, trying to get a university or a government agency to do a health study. Finally, county and state health agencies agreed at least to take a close look at cancer registries. It took them a year. When they came back to report the results, the initial condescension and annoyance we had sensed when they first agreed to look were gone. Yes, they told us, there is cancer at levels high enough and increasing fast enough to be concerned. In particular, we had high levels of lung, breast, brain, prostate, and cervical cancer. The rate for lung cancer in the county was the highest in the state. However, they said, the rates were not alarming. They just warranted close monitoring and more money for a local no-smoking campaign. Cancer rates also did not justify more money for a study.

What can you tell us about those who have cancer and their occupational backgrounds, we asked? Nothing. Is that important? Yes.

What can you tell us about cancer and length of residency, we asked? Nothing. Is that important? Yes.

In the autumn of 1995, I decided to be the someone I was waiting for. On long walks down country lanes, I had reflected on how to make sense of what was happening to me and those around me. If I was going to make my move, I had to have a context. I decided to tap the power of an "eco-human-health connection" I had been making in my mind. We'd do our own health survey. That way we could put some meat and bones on the state's study. Our own grassroots effort would encourage the government to do a more thorough and revealing study. If we could find out something about the characteristics of those who had cancer, maybe we would set some targets for that study. Our catalytic project would also raise issues about the use of the desert that were being ignored.

It began around a kitchen table. Karla Petersen had gone to school with my wife when Linda finished her degree through a local Utah State University extension program. She taught my kids algebra at the middle school. She has a wild sense of humor, boundless energy, and infectious enthusiasm, a strong mother-bear type who had battled and licked cancer twice before she reached her late thirties. Her younger brother was also fighting cancer. It was Karla's kitchen.

Sandy Covello was there. She was another mother bear, another energy junkie, and another tough survivor. She was outspoken and unafraid. She was widely known, well liked and respected, or at least loud enough that she couldn't be ignored. Janet Cook was older, a grandmother, and calmer, but also strong and determined. A former city councilwoman, she had been haranguing the county and state for years to no avail about how many cancers were clustered on her street. Among them, the three women knew just about everyone in town personally.

We drew up maps and listed possible recruits to go door to door, block by block. I left the logistics to them while I focused on the survey instrument, including what to ask, how to ask it, and what we could learn. I worked on definitions and methods. I found friendly professors at Brigham Young University to review the survey instrument and advise us. I suggested we call ourselves West Desert Healthy Environment Alliance. The short name would be West Desert HEAL. That expressed our approach and concern. We lived downwind from the West Desert. We wanted to heal. The first step would be to expose the community's wounds to cleansing light.

Early on, I realized that occupational history was beyond our scope. The individual histories would be so varied and complicated that they would require long interviews, much recording, complicated tabulations, and interviewing skills we couldn't assume or teach. But length of residency was relatively easy to establish and record. We were more interested in setting targets for a future study that would be prompted by our own modest effort than doing the exhaustive study ourselves and having the last word. The survey was also intended to raise consciousness and give people who were immobilized an activity to rally around. Together, we would shame the bureaucrats into action.

After Christmas, we were ready to roll. In all, about forty volunteers went door to door, asking questions, recording answers, and making maps of their neighborhoods. By February, half the town of 5,000 had been covered. Janet Cook was exhausted. No one else had covered more ground or done more to inspire and organize volunteers, check their progress, and collect their data. She became the leader. The survey became more than a full-time commitment for her; it was cathartic. Talking to neighbors and hearing the stories brought back by survey volunteers was heartbreaking and scary. At one point, she and her husband, Morley, called their extended family together and discussed the possibility of breaking their bond with the land their ancestors had made home and moving en masse to Montana.

I decided we had enough data to write a report. I wrestled with the raw material, then shared the numbers with my professor advisors and friends like Steve Erickson and Preston Truman of Downwinders who had done this kind of thing before and knew what to look for and how to present it. By the time I went to the annual Chemical Weapons Working Group conference in Washington DC that March, I had a rough draft of the survey report in hand and took it to Lee Davidson at the capitol offices of the *Deseret News*. The DesNews, as it is commonly called, is one of Salt Lake's two major daily newspapers and is owned by the Mormon Church. Lee is their Washington correspondent. He is a big, bright, soft-spoken man. He looked at our results and grilled me gently on our methods. His understanding of what happened upwind from us at Dugway is unsurpassed and he was sympathetic to our concerns. It was also a good story. Most journalists do not focus on the ideals of those who bring them stories because ideals don't sell stories. They look for real people in colorful settings who are engaged in interesting activities. I left with a promise to get our story on the front page of the Sunday paper when we were ready to release it.

When I returned home, I used Davidson's commitment to leverage interest from a producer at the local ABC television affiliate in Salt Lake. A "Cover Story" series was planned on "Utah's Northern Downwinders." The opening feature would air on the same Sunday the *Deseret News* did their story. With those two pieces of the media equation in place, it was easy to lure in all the other television stations and newspapers.

Newspapers and television stations like to scoop stories and are reluctant to present the stale news stories their competitors got to first. But they would rather be a close second than a stale third. I have learned that once you get a paper or television channel to go after a story, you can usually get its competitors to race it towards the deadline.

A roomful of HEAL volunteers gathered in Janet's living room a couple of days before the story broke to review the report, discuss our reactions, and go over how to handle reporters that might come our way. HEAL had no formal membership or elected leadership. There were people who wanted to help but couldn't muster the commitment to associate formally. They had neighbors, friends, and relatives who worked at Dugway, or Magcorp, or the chemical weapons incinerator, or in the West Desert Hazardous Industries Area and they didn't want to offend or threaten them. Rural Mormon culture has a narrow comfort zone for challenging authority. By keeping it loose and confidential, we could be more inclusive. That evening, however, we had a dozen volunteers who were moved by what they had learned on the street and were ready to speak out and act.

The report was released in early April of 1996. It said our survey confirmed the conventional wisdom that the health of Grantsville citizens is not good. We identified 201 cancers. The earlier cancer report issued by the Utah Bureau of Epidemiology listed a total of 237 cancers for Grantsville between 1973 and 1993 based on a search of cancer registries. Our survey turned up almost as many cancers as their research but we only surveyed about half of the town. Extrapolating that the rates for the other half of town we did not cover were similar to the half we did cover, one could assume approximately 200 additional cancers for a total close to 400. Even given a flawed methodology on our part, the two-to-one difference was remarkable. We readily conceded the inherent flaws in our layman's approach but also argued that it was just as likely that the state's dry statistical approach was inadequate when taken alone.

Most remarkably, the survey showed that the cancers we listed were highly concentrated among long-time residents. Of the 201 cancers we found, 182 were among natives (in the case of children) or long-time residents, those who reported they had lived in the county for at least twenty-five years. Census data on neighborhood mobility indicated that about one-third of Tooele County residents had lived in their neighborhoods for more than fifteen years. Even assuming that percentage could be higher in Grantsville, we still had to conclude that cancer was highly concentrated among a minority subset of residents, making the rates even more startling for that group. Although there is a definite correlation between length of residency and age, it could not be overstated. Many of the cancers reported among long-time residents occurred among those who were relatively young, in their thirties and early forties.

One hundred and eighty-one serious respiratory problems were reported. This number includes those diagnosed with asthma, emphysema, and "chronic" sinusitis. Asthma seemed epidemic. We did not include those who mentioned bronchitis, allergies, or pneumonia. Several elderly respondents mentioned shortness of breath and these were not included. Several newer residents said they had never had so many respiratory colds as they had experienced since moving to Grantsville. These were not included. Also, some volunteers focused primarily on cancer and practically ignored respiratory ailments. A more thorough and consistent effort would probably have turned up more respiratory problems.

Discovering reproductive problems and birth defects was difficult. Survey volunteers reported that people were, understandably, reticent about reporting on such personal aspects of their health. They suspect only a fraction of reproductive problems were reported and only a portion of birth defects. Thirty-eight reproductive problems were reported. Many more reported miscarriages but were not included unless they had a history of multiple miscarriages. The other problems included in this category were infertility and endometriosis. Interesting anecdotal information about miscarriages was revealed. Some respondents said they were aware of clusters of miscarriages in their neighborhoods, particularly in the 1950s and 60s when atomic testing in Nevada and chemical, biological, and radiological testing at Dugway was going on.

Twenty-nine serious birth defects were reported. These include cleft palates, spina bifida, and other serious disabilities. We heard about babies born with one kidney, a hole in the heart, or no brain. Again, the number of birth defects recorded was large but represented only a portion of the actual number in Grantsville since it included only half of the community. Interesting anecdotal evidence about birth defects also surfaced. One respondent, for example, reported that she gave birth to seriously deformed twins several months after the infamous sheep kill in Skull Valley in 1968. Her doctor told her he'd never seen so many birth defects as he did that year.

A number of other health problems were reported. These included eight cases of lupus, five non-cancer thyroid problems, ten cases of chronic fatigue syndrome, three other serious immune system problems, and four other neurological problems. Many people reported seizures but these were not included. We found twelve cases of multiple sclerosis. Combined with a cluster of MS identified by Joyce Stromberg in neighboring Tooele, the county had many times the number of MS sufferers one would expect to find in a normal population.

I did not want the survey report to be a plain accounting of the numbers. Data is not information, as information is not knowledge, and, as we have learned to our sorrow over and over this past century, knowledge is not wisdom. If a citizen's survey could not achieve the statistical credibility of a full-blown epidemiological study, it could at least recount the insights that only the people who live out their lives within a community can have. We believed it was the prerogative of a community to draw conclusions about its own wellbeing based on the unique, intimate, intuitive, and profound experiences of its members over time. Behind every number was a story. The stories told of the real-life experiences of individual human beings whose challenges and losses cannot be easily and neatly measured, tabulated, and compared.

Along with illness comes loss of capacity to work and to play treasured and sustaining roles as a family member. The ill lose social mobility and the ability to reach for cherished and validating goals. Illness is stressful and frightening. Illness is expensive. The suffering and loss of loved ones, friends, and neighbors goes way beyond those immediately affected. The ripple effects of poor public health extend throughout the community. Our survey taught us that the conditions and experience of individuals should never be reduced to mere statistics, means, averages, norms, margins for error, and valid sample sizes. Such measures are, after all, only tools to be applied for greater ends.

The way that government agencies set standards for allowable pollution seemed to us to be seriously flawed. What is deemed a tolerable amount of air pollution by the government is based on abstract and relative comparisons of pollution levels from one area to another. What is missing is the condition of the people on the ground who must breathe the air. Our survey showed that Grantsville residents were suffering and vulnerable. Further increases in emissions could not be tolerated. Enough, as determined by air quality regulators, is, in the case of a suffering and vulnerable population, too much. Pollution is not an act of God, nature, or fate. It is the result of human activity. It can be controlled, even stopped. We demanded a moratorium on new emission sources and a comprehensive plan for reducing existing air pollution.

The report conceded the possible occupational exposures Grantsville residents faced—the solvents at the army depot, chlorine gas at Magcorp, heavy metals and pollution at the Kennecott smelter, pesticides and herbicides from ranching. Even so, we concluded, occupational exposure is just one explanation. Environmental factors also had to be acknowledged and considered. Talking to older respondents revealed historical exposures I had not known about, like pollution from an old Tooele smelter that was closed before I moved in. Before Kennecott installed a taller smokestack, old timers said, pollution was worse from that source. An important record of exposure that had been overlooked was the testing and experimentation that was done at Dugway Proving Grounds from the 1950s through at least the 1970s. Despite Lee Davidson's thorough account of the Dugway tests, most of the residents we talked to during the survey had no idea such amounts of nerve agent, pathogens, radiation, and chemical simulants had been released. The report briefly described the hidden history of military testing and demanded that the sources of military pollution be completely documented and publicized.

Given the history of exposure to dangerous substances from army activities and the widespread and varied health problems revealed by the survey, important questions were raised about the army's credibility when they tell residents new activities are not dangerous. Betrayal of past trust is not a confidence builder. "Citizens," the report concluded, "would be well advised to be wary, monitor closely, and demand thorough evidence when new military activities are proposed. The incineration of nerve agent is particularly worrisome in light of past exposures and current health status. Technologies are often used without adequate assessment of their human and environmental impact, without democratic decision making about their use, and without the community's knowledge of their dangers. As individuals, we take personal responsibility for an aware, balanced, and proactive approach to our own behaviors that impact our health. As members of society, we must insist that decision makers and policy makers are accessible, accountable, and responsible."

Finally, our findings underscored fundamental and important understandings about our place as human beings within our environment. "We have learned," we stated at the end of the report, "that we are all downwind and downstream from one another. The environmental equivalent of the Biblical warning that we reap what we sow is that we also eat, breathe, and drink what we sow. As a society, we make collective choices about what we allow to enter our air and our food chain and we can no longer ignore that those decisions are eventually translated into flesh and blood and living experience. In Tooele County, Cold War imperatives and ambitions, the desire to preserve corporate profit, and a consensus about the need for jobs in a regional economy with limited options have often obscured those choices. No more. We are no longer willing to deny, rationalize, or justify environmental degradation. Clean air, water, and soil must be a priority because public health depends on them and we now stand warned."

Some of the most revealing aspects of our survey were hard to convey. There were many people in town who were ill but couldn't be placed in a category. Their suffering was hard to name. Don, a close friend of mine, is a case in point. In the course of a lifetime, he has been diagnosed with rheumatic fever, Riders disease, rheumatoid arthritis, lupus, chronic fatigue syndrome, and various blood disorders. None of these labels exactly describes his suffering and none provide a clear direction for treatment. In addition, he has had repeated surgery to replace his knee because of raging antibiotic-resistant infections that form around the artificial parts. He walks with a cane and his pain shows. In his mid-forties, ticket agents began asking him if he would like senior citizen discounts.

Don's multiple diagnoses reflect both the limits of pathological analysis and the condition of an immune system that has been badly compromised. People whose cellular chemistry has been scrambled by radioactive fallout, an occasional whiff of nerve agent, God only knows what pathogens, the episodic flow of chlorine gas through the air, and a dose of endocrine-disrupting dioxin, are likely to express the poor health that results kaleidoscopically. Genetic predisposition, exposure levels, exposure combinations, age, wealth, and individual mental and emotional states are all variables that mix into diverse symptoms and complaints.

Others who are sick never get labeled at all. Butch, another neighbor, was a big proud strong man until he suddenly became so tired and weak that he could no longer pull himself up on his horse to ride around his property and tend his cattle. He has spent weeks trapped in bed, too tired to crawl to the table, only to recover and go back to work until the next bout of fatigue occurs. A weary round of specialists and tests followed by experimentation with various drugs, each with its own peculiar set of side effects, has only added to his periodic exhaustion.

In the absence of a clear diagnosis, of course, it is easy to shift blame to the victim. What unresolved spiritual and emotional issues does the victim need to work out so he can recover? I don't know and maybe he doesn't either, but I am also willing to concede that sometimes illness is just a matter of being in the wrong place at the wrong time. Those who are ill are extremely sensitive to inferences that they are to blame for their own suffering. They often blame themselves. But the burden of being ill with no authoritative validation is itself an emotional issue that stands in the way of recovery.

Again, the impact of poor health cascades through a community in ways that are also not measurable. Don is a gifted teacher and coach, a good neighbor, a wise friend, and a thoughtful citizen. People like him, who share their knowledge and talents, make a contribution to a community that can't be replicated. Don has made a remarkable contribution despite his suffering, but he has also been frequently sidelined by pain. His losses are ours as well.

As for my personal parental concerns, the health survey confirmed my suspicion that widespread poor health was the result of historical exposures as well as occupational exposures. Native health was devastated by apocalyptic military activity. Dugway's mad testing phase was over by the time we moved in. Above-ground atomic testing was over, too. My kids were probably not in harm's way, any more than any American kid who drinks milk, plays in the dirt, and breathes. But the survey also reminded me of the potential risks of living on the rim of the Great Basin. There would be dioxins from two commercial hazardous waste incinerators and a chemical weapons incinerator. One accident at the latter could put us all under a cloud of suffering like the Peck family or the Dugway workers. Hazardous waste would be trucking by our house on its way to the WDHIA. Dioxins from Magcorp were an unknown piece of the puzzle. All the ingredients were present for a next generation of downwinders.

Whatever could be conveyed about the community's health, whether in raw numbers or intangible subtleties, was my job. I worked doggedly to keep the report in the spotlight to pressure state officials into meeting our demands. The response justified my effort. Nothing puts an issue on the agenda of bureaucrats like two minutes on the nightly television news. Instead of being contacted by lowly functionaries, I was getting personal phone calls from executive directors of departments. How can we meet your needs, they asked politely? Of course, at the same time state scientists and doctors were tearing our survey to shreds behind our backs.

The ensuing controversy over whose numbers were correct and the criticism of our methodology missed the point. Whether the state's figures for cancer were correct or our totals were, our survey at least showed that illness of all kinds was concentrated among long-term residents who had been living in the area when Dugway was testing or those whose parents were present then. That part seemed undeniable to me. The implications of this were also missed. If we do not have reliable information on what low-level exposure to nerve agent does to health over time, then Grantsville's case might be thought provoking. Here was a group that was exposed and twenty years later they were ill. But the exposure could not be proved because nobody was tracking it. We just assumed that if you put 3.5 trillion lethal doses into the open air upwind from a population they had to encounter some of it. As usual, there were all the complicating variables to consider.

The discussion about a health study went on for months. A baseline study was finally agreed to but never funded. I didn't care. By that time I was sure we would never conclude anything with a health study. I was burned out on looking backward and convinced the government was not up to doing meaningful work for us. I remembered the words of the walking wounded in San Diego, "inconclusive by design." Now I understood.

What was useful was already in hand. The connection between environmental quality and health was made and was now part of the public agenda. Public health got a place at the table when decisions were made about our environment. We changed the terms of public discourse. From that point on, no local politician could suggest adding one more smoke-stack industry to the county without knowing there would be tough questions and real opposition. We hadn't reversed course, but the brakes were now on and we were ready for fixed targets.

Although it is hard to measure, many participants in the HEAL survey reported a powerful shift in consciousness. We do not like to think of ourselves as bodies, as physical beings that express ecosystems we do not control and do not under-stand. We like to think of ourselves as moms and dads, teachers and lawyers, entrepreneurs and workers, coaches and neigh-bors, Anglos and Latinos, Christians and Jews. Defining and identifying ourselves through our family and community rela-tionships, our careers, our ethnicity, and our beliefs is natural and to be expected. But there is also a habit of mind in our culture that divides the "self" that names from the human body that contains it, and the human body from the "ecobody" that, in turn, contains it. This habit of mind is broken as soon as one becomes ill. Then you experience the shocking understanding that you may be a Republican attorney, a Catholic grandfather, and an Orioles fan, but you are also a heart, lungs, lymph nodes, colon, testicles, and skin. Unfortunately, getting ill, or having someone you are close to become ill, is often what it takes to wake up and see what is at stake.

Much is written and heard lately about the power of mind and prayer on sound health and healing. We are beginning to understand how physical healing can require the resolution of personal and philosophical issues, past experiences, and primary relationships. All of that may be so, but the body is still vulnerable and compelling, especially when it is threatened. There is ample evidence that we are rediscovering our bodies, but the signals are mixed. As more and more of us take up running, walking, biking, aerobics, yoga, vitamins, herbs, and organic local diets, more of us are getting fatter and getting fatter younger. Even so, the urge towards body awareness and health is promising and powerful. The eco-human-health connection teaches us that health also depends on collective attitudes and behaviors.

Increasing numbers of people have been touched by illness they suspect has environmental causes. Although they are particularly receptive to eco-human-health messages, the complications and difficulties of activating a group of ill people are significant since they are preoccupied and debilitated by their illnesses. But the circle of this constituency is much broader than those immediately affected and, sadly, is ever expanding and becoming more inclusive. It includes caregivers, families, and neighbors. It includes anyone with an imagination and a proactive concern for his or her own health. Parents who care deeply about risks to the health of their children will be especially motivated to ask what risks are fair and acceptable and for what ends.

Each environmental health issue has its own set of players, rules, and circumstances and can be played out on that level alone. Environmental issues are always about democracy, about creating decision-making processes that are inclusive, open, accountable, and informed. They are about who gets to sit at the decision-making table. The rules govern behavior, so power over rules is important. Power over goals is also key because the goals also guide behavior.

Beyond gaining the power to change goals and rules, however, the most far-reaching changes happen when basic assumptions, values, and meanings are challenged. The goals and rules come from a mindset or paradigm that is always transparent in the sense that it is assumed and self-reinforcing. The eco-human-health connection is a new way of looking at the world from bottom to top. It is a means of changing both individual and collective behavior by reminding people that they are rooted in their bodies, which are rooted in an ecosystem that is rooted in yet broader and more inclusive natural systems. When social behaviors and political action are motivated by the desire to defend one's own body, and that body is firmly located in an ecosystem, then the goals and rules that are now focused by concerns about profits, jobs, taxes, and our culture's various acquisitive addictions will change. To the insightful slogan "think globally, act locally," the eco-human-health approach adds "think culturally, act bodily." Embodiment demands empowerment.

HEAL members decided that the open burning and detonation of conventional munitions was a likely target. For forty years townsfolk tolerated the chicken squawking, dog barking, baby crying, boom-boom rhythm of "detonation season" because we knew it was the sound of employment and economic security. The Tooele Army Depot had recently closed, or "realigned" as they insisted on calling it. Most of the jobs left for other depots but the munitions, chemical and otherwise, stayed behind. They still detonated and we didn't have to take it any more. For a year prior to the survey, a small group of us called and complained to the army directly and to the state agencies that regulated detonation. After the survey, it was easier to get people to call and write and attend hearings. We had more credibility. I no longer spoke as an individual but as a "spokesperson" for West Desert HEAL.

Still, people lacked faith in their ability to make change. So the first step was simply to break our silence and show others they could speak up without repercussions. We talked about how unusual it was to have huge amounts of military ordinance blowing sky high every few hours during daylight hours from March through October every year. We complained openly about how "bombing" cracked the plaster in our homes and rattled our windows loose. We wondered aloud whether the clouds of dust that often blew our way after explosions contained harmful heavy metals or phosphorous. We distributed phone numbers that people could call at the depot to complain and whenever an explosion shook us we made the commander's phone ring off the hook. Linda worked in town at the elementary school, so she kept track of the explosions and led the phone-in campaign. She distributed the phone numbers of the Utah Division of Air Quality and urged people to call them. Finally, once the speak-out ball was rolling, we asked people to call local elected officials to ask why they weren't doing something to alleviate our problems.

We did not begin by demanding an end to open detonation. Instead, we pursued a series of small and winnable goals. Each was reasonable and doable. First we demanded that the depot blow up smaller loads in deeper detonation pits to lesson the concussive impacts. They agreed. We asked the Division of Air

Quality to find out what was in those clouds of dirt. We asked the depot only to detonate on days when the wind blew away from us until the contents of the dirt plumes were known. They agreed. When their tests of the plume were questionable, we challenged the results. When we found out they could analyze weather conditions before detonating so that conditions were optimal for minimum noise, we insisted on that rule and got it. When we found out we could file claims for damages to property from detonation, we did. Finally, we asked them to move part of their detonation activity to a remote location and they did. Our demands targeted the rules and had a cumulative impact.

All along the way, we tied our complaints to a larger compelling context, our concern about poor health in the community. One of our leaders was a woman confined to a wheelchair with an oxygen tank strapped to the back. She was a constant reminder of the stress and struggle of those downwind to cope with what was coming at them from the depot's detonation pits. Defining the problem is a key to success. Polluters will always try to define the problem technically and then set their hired experts and lawyers against the limited time and resources of citizens. So keeping the big picture up front is important.

Under pressure, the army moved detonation to the South Area of the Tooele Army Depot, about fifteen miles away from Grantsville. A year later, when the chemical weapons incinerator fired up, it was moved back. By then the army saw the writing on the wall and the depot went to "Tier One" status, meaning it only stores "fresh" munitions to be used in the first ninety days of a conflict. Fresh munitions mean there is little need to blow up the stale old stuff. Today, less than one-fifth of the amount of munitions that have traditionally been detonated at the Tooele Army Depot are destroyed and alternatives to any open-air detonation are being explored. The number of detonation pits has been doubled so the loads blown-up are a fraction of what they once were. All the rules and guidelines that were established over the three years we leaned on them still apply. The quiet summer of 1997 was the first concussion-lite summer Grantsville experienced in forty years.

As people find their voice and start to win, an amazing change happens. People gain confidence about their own abilities to think and judge. Authorities and their hired experts lose credence. Unexpected creative energies are tapped in common folks. Watching this is one of the joys of activism.

Our sleepy little rural town did not become a hot bed of radical environmentalism. But after decades of ineffective complaint, fatalistic acceptance, and denial, we got the whole town talking and many people became determined for the first time ever to do something. Soon after the survey, the safety of the nearby chemical weapons incinerator was being openly debated despite the fact that hundreds of neighbors earned their livings there. Another major employer, the Magcorp magnesium refinery north of town, also lost its untouchable status and was soon being challenged.

The survey was widely read and reported along the Wasatch Front, the cluster of booming suburbs stretching north and south of Salt Lake City. It became a catalyst for organizing along the Wasatch Front against the chemical weapons incinerator and Magcorp. Those who read about it took little comfort in the fact that the numbers came from Grantsville. The wind does not obey political jurisdictions. They knew they were reading a warning. The people in Grantsville were like the canaries kept in coalmines in the old days to warn miners of the presence of dangerous fumes.

Regulators do not regulate effectively, legislators do not legislate boldly, policy and decision-makers do not make wise choices, and corporations do not budge from their bottom line if citizens do not show up, speak up, and take action. The heroes and heroines of the environmental movement are the "little people" who come home after work or school, grab a bite to eat, and charge off to meetings and hearings. They write letters after the kids are tucked into bed, or take an afternoon off to lobby a legislator or attend a rally. Contrary to cynical conventional wisdom, they do make a big difference. When they are not around, bad things can happen to good people.

Constantly showing up and challenging the rules, however, is going to be endless and exhausting as long as the rules of the current regulatory regime remain as is. To get beyond these endless battles while the world burns, we must change the rules fundamentally. To do that, minds must change. Spreading the gospel of eco-human-health is one compelling way of changing minds because it does not just focus on the rules of environmental politics but on the context that creates the rules. The messages of eco-human-health raise the stakes in the struggle for a clean environment powerfully and personally. Underlining how environmental ills contribute to human illness is as scientifically sound and defensible as the current emphasis on heredity and behavior. Sure your genes make a difference. Sure diet and exercise and habits like smoking are important factors. But environmental factors are also keys to health and we ignore them at our peril.

The newsletter I wrote and the information packets I distributed at every opportunity I could find, first for HEAL and then for its Wasatch Front cousin, Families Against Incinerator Risk, stressed hard news about specific campaigns, but also hammered on basic themes. Again and again, I said the most direct link you have with your environment is your own body and its health. Your body, I explained, is composed of more than a trillion cells that are constantly renewed. Every year of your life you have a new liver, new marrow, new stomach lining, and so on. Breast cells turn over monthly. New cells have to come from somewhere and they come from the food we eat, the fluids we drink, and the air we breathe. Our environment becomes us as soil, plant, animal, water, and air are processed into flesh and blood.

If these basic lessons are self-evident, we do not act as though they are. Our culture from one end of the spectrum to the other tells us we are what we think. Fundamentalist Christians and starry-eyed New Agers share this mind over matter theme. Scientists make much of their empirical approach but also live in their Cartesian heads. In important ways, we are what we think and become who we think we are. But in very real, demonstrable, and self-evident ways we are also what we eat, breathe, and drink. Healing the body and healing disconnected consciousness go hand in hand. They are the yin and yang of the environmental movement.

Each year there is a breast cancer awareness week sponsored by a major pharmaceutical company that makes a profit selling drugs to women who are undergoing treatment for breast cancer. They are in the breast cancer business. The slogan of the campaign is "detection is the best prevention." How absurd! By the time you detect breast cancer you can't prevent it because you already have it. The subtext of this slogan is "cancer is inevitable," so don't look for causes. Early treatment is all you can do. This is an example of how twisted the conventional thinking is on health and the environment. It is like telling a boiling frog "heat is inevitable, so just do the best you can to endure it."

If you eat mindfully, organically, and low on the food chain, exercise often, avoid bad habits, keep a positive outlook, and are lucky enough to inherit healthy genes, you are in the best position to ward off any illness that comes your way. But if you ignore the numerous environmental hazards in your community's ecosystem, if you are ignorant of the pathways pollution has into your body, you have still not done everything you can to defend your health. You and your loved ones are still at risk. Collective behaviors are also important to health.

We need millions of ecodetectives, investigating the hazards and risks in their backyards and making the connection between poor health and environmental degradation. We must insist loud and clear that sound health is a self-evident right and that needless risk is unfair. Be a smart frog and recognize the sick canary when you see it. Then jump!

EIGHT

KISSING THE ARMY'S ASS ON THE COURTHOUSE STEPS AT HIGH NOON

"Are you the guy I see on TV talking against the incinerator?" It was a phone call out of the blue on a Saturday night in August 1994. I had hoped I could relax.

"Yeah," I said warily, "who are you?" I expected an argument. I wanted a beer.

"Steve Jones," the voice said. "I am the chief safety officer at Tooele Incinerator, or at least I was until EG&G fired me on Wednesday." Suddenly, I was all ears. The man seemed alarmed. Months later he told me he had received his first death threat by the time he called me. He needed to get his story out fast for insurance. It was quite a story.

Jones had been a top safety inspector for the navy and won their most prestigious award for safety inspection two years in a row. He'd been tapped by the holy of holies in the inspection world, the inspector general's office. Clearly a star in the military realm he moved in, Jones decided to make the classic move people in such careers make. He accepted a job with a defense contractor, EG&G. EG&G had built a billion-dollar fortune and reputation by running the underground nuclear weapons testing site in Nevada. They also tackled such diverse military tasks as salvaging a broken nuclear sub from the sea floor and operating the chemical weapons incinerator in Utah. Jones knew all about the chemical weapons demilitarization program and the plans to build eight massive incinerators across the nation to get rid of chemical weapons that are now banned by an international treaty. He had inspected all the major chemical weapons stockpiles and had access to all the documentation and communication the program generated. Or, at least he thought he knew the program.

He described his first weeks at the Tooele Chemical Disposal Facility, or TOCDF, incinerator as a series of shocks. TOCDF on paper and TOCDF under his nose couldn't have been more at odds. On paper, the plant was safe, clean, and efficient. Up close, he told me, it was "a bomb ready to go off."

At the core of the incinerator's problems was a history of design failure. The military's original scheme for getting rid of chemical armaments was the CHASE—"cut holes and sink 'em"—scheme, where old ships were loaded with the evil stuff, towed out to sea, and then sunk. When this method was perceived as an obvious bad idea, Congress described and funded a process that was logically designed. Congress's original intent for the chem demil program was sound, regardless of the technological means chosen to do the job. First, they said, build a prototype facility, the smallest burner called CAMDS for Chemical Agent Munitions Disposal System, that is located right next door to TOCDF. Learn from the prototype and then redesign. Next, build a larger pilot plant, the one in the South Pacific known as JACADS, or Johnston Atoll Chemical Agent

Disposal System. Learn again and redesign. Finally, build a full-scale bomb burner in Utah where the lion's share of chemical weaponry is stored. That scenario for design and implementation could be characterized as "start—better—best." It makes sense.

That's not how it happened. The PMCD gang, or Program Manager for Chemical Demilitarization as it was officially called, unfortunately demonstrated the organizational wherewithal of the Keystone Cops. The Cold War against the Evil Empire was in full swing. No one was watching. They built their prototype based on what was known about combustion technology in the late seventies–early eighties. Then, incineration was cutting edge, at least compared with dumping garbage off a barge. Since then, more than 240 proposed incinerators have been defeated by nearby communities as incineration has accumulated a reputation for poisonous emissions. So the Pentagon may have climbed on the wrong train to begin with. But even had they picked a different technology to do the job, they guaranteed a troubled design. Before the CAMDS prototype was tested out, they designed and then built JACADS. Before JACADS was tested out, they designed and built TOCDF. Instead of "start—better—best," they had "small—medium—large" of the same basic plant design, with all the problems and flaws passed along from one plant to the next. What Jones found on the rim of the Great Basin in Utah was an enormous Rube Goldberg contraption with hundreds of add-ons and complicated modifications. In his first couple of months on the job, he found thousands of safety violations, including 150 that were in a safety category for those that could portend "imminent catastrophic" consequences.

The MITRE Corporation had been hired to do an independent audit of safety just before Jones arrived. The MITRE report described 3,016 design deficiencies and pointed out that federally mandated hazard analyses of design flaws had not been done. Jones' own analysis agreed. While preparing for a visit by the Inspector General's office, Jones toured the facility with a critical and professional eye. He was particularly upset by conditions he saw in the "unpack area" where munitions are stripped of packing and prepared for processing. It was "worse than the Three Stooges," he said, with workers wrestling rockets with crowbars. "The worst man–machine interface I have ever seen."

There were few standard operating procedures for complicated high-risk tasks. There was minimal safety training and next to no compliance with safety regulations. The plant was already falling apart. Workers walked through this safety minefield in shifts, so that for one week a guy was on days, then swing, then graveyard. Shift rotation was more cost effective for EG&G. Productivity demands pushed safety aside at every turn. Jones called it "death by design."

How could this happen? "There are two armies here," he explained, and one was not accountable. The "regular" army had effective rules and procedures for handling chemical munitions. Their reputation was solid. But that army was under a separate command. The Program Manager for Chemical Demilitarization, PMCD, operated outside the normal army pecking order. PMCD, or "chem demil," could exempt itself from army rules and was accountable only to the Secretary of Defense. As for the state of Utah's role in monitoring and regulating the incinerator, Jones thought state agencies had simply "rolled over" to the army and it was too late to expect more from them because mistakes would have to be admitted, misjudgments conceded. If the state admitted it had been hasty or easy, reputations would be tarnished and careers ruined. In the final analysis, Jones argued, independent oversight by people who understand safety, engineering, and chemical weapons is called for. He was going to sound the alarm.

If workers inside the plant were ill-prepared to handle the daunting risks they faced, the situation outside the gates was no better. The Chemical Stockpile Emergency Planning Program, or CSEPP, was charged with preparing the public for accidents and emergencies and had already achieved a scandalous reputation for squandering millions of dollars with nothing to show for it. Local emergency responders were untrained and unequipped. They didn't even have protective clothing. In the event of a leak, how would police get out there to direct traffic? Their mission would be suicidal without protective clothing. Would citizens who jump in their cars to flee know they were supposed to turn left at the dead sheriff? Several poles with loudspeakers on them were erected in surrounding communities to give instructions in case of an emergency. No one could hear the speakers from inside their homes and cars and they became targets for bored kids with guns who found them more challenging to hit than the usual targets, cattle crossing signs. Calendars had been distributed with advice on stocking up food and water. Years later, in March of 1998, a CBS *60 Minutes* report claimed that the Oregon emergency preparedness program was no better than its Utah predecessor and had blown $600 million with nothing to show for it.

Jones knew that the army liked to use GB, or Sarin, nerve

gas for its disbursement models and emergency scenarios because it was light and dissipated quickly compared with its oily persistent cousin, VX. If VX got loose out there, he knew there would be more casualties than local emergency responders and hospitals could handle after the best training and preparedness campaign, and this was far from best. There was scant coordination with local government. He asked the mayor of a nearby community how he'd respond if casualties came his way and the man replied, "I'll blow the bridge up."

When Jones tried to document his scary discoveries, TOCDF's general manager, Henry Silvestri, went ballistic and told him never to put bad news in writing. Bad news delivered verbally was always met with the same excuse, "we're not hot yet." "Okay," Jones replied, "you're not hot, but you're stupid."

When Jones was told to sign off on a document proclaiming that the 3,016 design deficiencies identified in the MITRE report posed an "acceptable risk" and that no corrective action was required, he balked. He knew that by law he was personally and financially liable if anyone died or was hurt from one of those flaws. Silvestri was adamant and admonished him to learn to "please the customer," in this case the PMCD army. Silvestri said, according to Jones, "If you have to kiss the army's ass at high noon on the courthouse steps, let me know and I'll come hold your hat." Jones stood his ground until they pulled the rug out from under him. His private sector career had lasted less than three months.

He was shocked and offended. "As soon as my friends in the Pentagon find out what is really going on out here," he told me over the phone, "they'll be on a plane for Utah the next day and shut that plant down."

"You must know a different army than the one I know," I replied, "because the army I know is going to smear your good name from one end of the nation to the other and you'll never work in the defense industry again."

My efforts to persuade him to get a lawyer were confidently rebuffed. He didn't need one. He was right. EG&G was wrong. He had credibility in high places and that was all that would be needed, as if billions of dollars in contracts, careers, and reputations were not at stake. He wanted to tell his story and he wanted to talk to the Citizen's Advisory Committee that was charged with watching over the incinerator. Could I make it happen?

I hung up the phone and called a local television reporter at home in Park City. When he called back to say he had an appointment with Jones in the morning, I called another reporter and told him the first reporter I called was ahead of him. I did not have to work hard to get reporters racing each other to the story. Within days it had attracted national interest. Throughout the ensuing media circus, Jones continued to display an innocence that astonished me. At one point I called to tell him I had a phone message from CNN. "Who are they?" he asked. I explained. "Oh, I don't have cable," he said and added, "I have a phone message from somebody who works for a guy named Peter Jennings. Who is he?"

The Citizen's Advisory Committee, or CAC, had been appointed by Utah governor Michael Leavitt to monitor the incinerator program in Utah. Although 45 percent of the munitions, or about 10,000 tons, were in our state and we had both the prototype incinerator and the first full-scale burner, Utah was the next to last state to appoint a CAC. I had campaigned for one and often explained to the public officials I managed to corner that it would be a place for whistleblowers to come to. The Tooele County commissioners couldn't be persuaded. They didn't want any pesky bunch of pointy-headed people looking over their shoulders while they negotiated with the army over impact fees for the county treasury. They were in the guv's political party and he respected their wishes, until Commissioner Gary Griffith began acting like the head pimp in an environmental red light district.

The county's aging hospital was experiencing rough times. Its performance and reputation were anemic and it needed a transfusion of funding the county couldn't afford. Griffith offered to take all the chemical munitions from all the other stockpile communities across the nation to burn in Tooele County if he could have several million dollars for a new hospital. He was clearly ready to take bids. It wasn't that Griffith was willing to trade environmental quality and public health for bucks that alarmed Leavitt. After all, county and state officials had crossed that line long ago. But he was offering to make deals with too few zeroes in them. Eventually, county commissioners would get $114 million in property and about $13 million in cash for just letting the Utah part of the program go forward. They would use the money to build a county recreation complex that would include a rodeo stadium, a demolition derby stadium, a mining museum, and howitzer rides. After Griffith threw his "what-am-I-bid" bomb, Leavitt had seen enough and appointed a CAC to provide one more means of monitoring the incinerator. Jones' appearance before the committee was its first test.

It failed with flying colors. To placate the offended Tooele

County commissioners, who rightly perceived the appointment of the CAC as an implied judgement about their inability to monitor the incinerator program on their own, the CAC was packed with those friendly to the program and in bed with commissioners. They received Jones coldly, grilled him, and then attacked him. CAC member Sid Hullinger said he'd be more inclined to listen to Jones if he had not created so much publicity around himself, as if whistleblower protection should only go to those whistleblowers who have surrendered or suppressed their First Amendment rights. Jones, he said, was just "disgruntled." Nobody on the CAC thought to point out that Hullinger's trucking firm was well positioned to do business with the incinerator and he might be agitated and disgruntled by those who could throw cold water on a lucrative prospect. No one pointed out that Gary Griffith's construction firm made piles of money building incinerators. Self-interest, apparently, was subject to a double standard and only applied to the fired safety manager.

Steve Jones was shocked again. The CAC's hostile reception was unexpected. A week later, a team of investigators from the Pentagon who flew out to check on the Jones charges issued a report saying the safety problems at TOCDF were what you'd expect to see in an industrial operation going through a shakedown before firing up. The community Jones was trying to protect more than shunned him. He had to change his phone number and ask the police to patrol his house. He got a lawyer.

It was a shame the CAC found whistleblowers embarrassing and upsetting. Over the next few years a whistleblowers' parade would march out the incinerator's back door. In 1996, the plant's general manager, a long time EG&G loyalist who was called in to run the place after the Jones story broke and Henry "kiss their ass" Silvestri took a hasty retirement, also went public with complaints about a lax safety culture at TOCDF. Gary Millar compared the situation at the bomb burner with those that preceded the Challenger disaster, Bhopal, and Three Mile Island. That same year, John Hall, a conscientious employee, claimed he was harassed out of his job when he complained about lax safety.

In 1997, it was Trina Allen's turn. She was the chief of hazardous waste operations, no small responsibility in a process that produces fifteen pounds of hazardous waste for every pound of agent burned. According to Allen, she had witnessed numerous unsafe and noncompliant activities, like the time a toxic spill in a storage yard was snowplowed against a boundary fence and left. More seriously, she had documentation showing arsenic in the burner's waste stream. Arsenic could only show up if the chemical agent Lewisite was being burned, and TOCDF was not set up to burn Lewisite and specifically prohibited from doing so. If an accident occurred while they were burning the unpermitted agent and it was released into the facility or the atmosphere, there would be no way to know and no alarms would warn. Allen guessed the Lewisite was hiding at the bottom of one-ton containers that had been incompletely drained of Lewisite before being refilled with GB nerve agent, or Sarin as it was popularly called after a weird religious cult released it in a Tokyo subway. The army and EG&G vehemently denied her claims when she made them and then, months later after the controversy disappeared from the news, they quietly admitted they had indeed burned Lewisite. They figured it came from contaminated one-ton containers as she had charged.

Jones eventually went to court. EG&G's team of high-priced lawyers orchestrated a festival of Jones bashers, company men desperate to show their loyalty, who charged Jones kept a stuffed monkey in his office and made fun of bald guys. No wonder he was fired. Besides, they argued, the Pentagon checked out the charges and found no problems. The trial of Steve Jones revealed in serial fashion the corporate culture of EG&G. As I sat in the courtroom watching, I imagined working in a backstabbing environment where employees jockeyed desperately for advantage in an ever-shifting pecking order. Engineering knowledge and technical skill were secondary to displays of loyalty to the corporation and cunning in office politics. These are the guys we are trusting to burn nerve gas in our backyard, I thought. These are the guys we are trusting to be honest about the risks we face. One EG&G officer who thought Jones was too strict explained that the company's career men were used to running the nuclear war test facility in Nevada. Burning nerve gas was no big deal compared with blowing up megaton nuclear devices underground.

Steve's Greenlaw and Government Accountability Project lawyers, whose automobiles cost less than the three-piece suits worn by the opposition's attorneys, put up a valiant fight. The EG&G and army documents that were brought to light during the discovery process of the Jones trial and later, during subsequent legal battles, were revealing. For example, the work diary of Don Smith, a quality assurance specialist at the incinerator, painted a portrait of safety officers struggling to be heard and taken seriously by superiors who constantly ignored or overruled them in favor of faster production and lower costs. "What is happening at TOCDF," he wrote in 1997, "is not risk management, it is gambling. Risk management is the informed assumption of risk. Gambling is taking uninformed risk and hoping everything will be OK without the slightest understanding of what the real issues are. TOCDF has been in this gambling mode since the project began."

To be most effective, the written record had to be backed by witnesses and it was not easy generating witnesses among his former coworkers who had to walk the EG&G plank to get to the courthouse. Towards the end of the trial, a friendly witness was visited by army personnel who intimidated him into silence. Outraged lawyers asked for an FBI investigation and went home angry. Then everybody waited, and waited, and waited.

Finally, in August of 1997, almost three years to the day from the date he was fired, a federal judge ruled that EG&G should reinstate Jones in his job and pay him back pay plus a half-million dollars compensation. Or, they could refuse to reinstate him and cough up back pay plus a million dollars. In describing EG&G's testimony and reasoning before her court, Judge Ellen Shea used words like "mendacity," "charade," "pretext," "lie," "incredible," and "unbelievable." Impressed by the judge's tone, the *Salt Lake Tribune* issued an editorial that questioned the credibility and integrity of those trusted to burn nerve agent upwind from us. Jones had kicked the army's ass at high noon on the courthouse steps. I was proud to hold his hat.

Nevertheless, EG&G stubbornly appealed. Two appeals boards agreed with the original decision, though the last one told the giant defense contractor just to reinstate Jones with back pay, period. If they wanted Jones out, they could figure out what it was worth to them and deal with him directly. In early 1999, EG&G was still stalling and belligerent. Steve Jones was eager to get back inside TOCDF, now renamed Deseret by their PR team after the original Mormon name for Utah, and tackle the safety issues he had abruptly left more than four years earlier, even if he had to wear a bullet-proof vest to do it. In May, he got his job back. Well, maybe. EG&G changed faces and treated him like royalty but recorded his every move and informed him he would have to be "retrained and recertified" to bring him up to speed, a process that could drag on for many months.

Steve Jones and his wife paid heavily for his uncompromising principles and his desire to protect public health. He spent four years that could have been his prime career earning years huddled with attorneys, talking on the phone, and trying to hustle a living selling used appliances and real estate. When his benefits were interrupted, their health suffered. The stress of the suit and the financial turmoil they were thrown into eventually tore them apart and they divorced. He sacrificed his career, his wealth, and his marriage.

Steve made the best of his new unanticipated life outside the military's gates. He visited several stockpile communities and spoke bravely about his experiences to appreciative audiences. He provided incineration opponents with valuable insights into the plant's operation and management. He became a hero among a circle of people he had probably spent most of his life dismissing as scruffy rabble-rousing rebels.

I sat in a bar with him in DC during the first CWWG conference he attended and caught him looking around at his ecoactivist drinking companions with amused wonder. Here was a man who had burrowed deep into the clean-cut by-the-book world of the military bureaucracy, moving from missile silo to chemical weapons stockpile, easy with the language and assumptions of Cold War hawks. He toiled in the forest of mass destruction, detailing the trees and rarely looking up to see the landscape he now faced daily. Here he was in a tavern, surrounded by a loose bunch of former hippies and housewives who were shouting at the very gates that had insulated him and his Pentagon colleagues. He was a man whose life had taken a sharp and unexpected turn that landed him in strange company. He had given up a beloved career and a way of life that he liked because he wouldn't give up his principles. He was supposed to protect people, not put them at risk. He was supposed to do his job right. He was too proud and strong-willed to bend to anything less.

Trina Allen also went to court and won. EG&G appealed and lost again. Millar didn't have to go to court. EG&G gave him a bankroll and let him keep his company truck. Unlike Jones and Allen, he had been with them for many years. We can only guess what else he knew. John Hall is still fighting his case. The CWWG set up a 1-800 hotline number for whistle-blowers. They hear regularly from anonymous employees who tell tales of incompetence and cover-up.

Two years after Jones was banished for saying the plant was accident prone, but only seventy-two hours after the Utah incinerator went hot and started burning live agent in August of 1996, it leaked and was shut down. The leak illustrated Steve's critique of the plant perfectly. It occurred in the same area near filter banks that was a problem at the JACADS pilot plant. By the time the demil boys knew they had a "migration" problem along that wall at JACADS, it was too late to do anything about the design of TOCDF. So they built a bandage line of wooden sheds over the vulnerable area at TOCDF and packed it with insulation and monitoring equipment. Sure enough, the Utah plant went hot and leaked right where they expected it to. In the wake of the first leak, serious questions were raised about whether state and local officials responsible for public safety were informed of the problem in a timely and prescribed manner. This also followed a pattern established at JACADS where bad news took weeks, even months, to come to light if at all. It also set a new pattern for TOCDF where critical questions would soon be raised about leaks and cover-ups.

In typical army fashion, they painted a smiley face on the side of their failure and proudly proclaimed no agent had escaped during an event that, they claimed, was typical of a "start-up" period. Just days before they stood in court and assured a federal judge that they should be trusted to fire up their incinerator because they had already shaken all the bugs out during a test burn phase.

For those who live in the army's backyard, such two-faced behavior is too routine. They mislead by habit and inclination, a secretive reflex they acquired during the long Cold War. BS was the raw material for their PR. For example, the army's rush to burn was always based on the argument that the stockpile of chemical weapons in their arsenal was deteriorating and becoming unstable. Projectiles were beginning to leak and the M-55 rockets in particular were in danger of spontaneously combusting as the propellant within them broke down. There was no time for second thoughts, they claimed, let alone for the development of safer alternatives to incineration. In the early years of their campaign to capture the cooperation of citizens in stockpile communities, the army's PR advance team carried with them a video of a bunker filled with M-55s exploding into an ominous black-orange cloud of lethal smoke. Imagine this happening, they told their innocent audiences, just down the road from your home.

Their claim that the M-55 rocket propellant could start blowing up in as little as fifteen years, however, was based on a mistake. In the formula for how fast propellant breaks down, days were conveniently confused with weeks and the estimate was off by a factor of seven. They discovered this miscalculation on their own, but chose not to share it until activists with the CWWG also found out and went public in the summer of '94. Information on the leaking nature of the stockpile was also manipulated, selected, and exaggerated to convey a crisis that left no time for alternatives. While belittling critics' fears of incineration emissions and leaks, PMCD never failed to wear its Chicken Little hat when discussing the condition of the stockpile. Opponents took for granted that every time bad news about incineration appeared, it would be followed by news of leaking containers detected in storage bunkers.

Questions about how fast the stockpile is deteriorating raised other more interesting questions for me when I first researched what was hiding in my backyard. Living in Grantsville, I was well aware that old munitions become unstable and have to be destroyed. That's why we had booming summers as stale munitions were openly detonated in pits south of town. The fact that old munitions become unstable has been well known since Napoleon. The hardest part of destroying old chemical weapons, all agree, is "reconfiguring" the stockpile. That is, engineering ways to separate explosive propellant from nerve agent so each can be disposed of appropriately. There is no easy way just to unscrew one component and divide it from the other. Each class of munitions, from rockets to land mines, presents its own unique separation problems. Some are punched and drained, others cut in two.

So, if the inevitability of dangerous deterioration is a given, and there is no simple or consistent way of separating nerve agent from propellant in the munitions, one must conclude that a design flaw of breathtaking proportion was built into the arsenal. That, or the military minds that conceived our massive collection of chemical weaponry were so convinced they would use them that they did not consider the possibility of the weapons getting old enough to warrant destruction. Given the uncontrollable and indiscriminate nature of nerve agent, as demonstrated at Dugway, their willingness to imagine using such weapons of mass destruction struck me as madness. Stupid or crazy? Take your pick. Not exactly a confidence builder, either way.

If the rush to burn was based on deterioration, and the M-55s are unquestionably the most dangerous of the lot, then M-55s must be handled first. But the M-55 "campaign" at TOCDF ran into problems right away. Just as they had at the JACADS pilot, the rockets tended to jam in the feed gates of the "deactivation" furnace. When burned, unacceptable and illegal amounts of PCBs were released into the open airstream. In March of '97, the M-55 campaign was abandoned so they could rethink their methods. The public was not notified for seven months.

The chem demil program was twelve years behind schedule before the Utah burner was fired up. Even more time was lost during the stumbling M-55 campaign. Although one-ton containers filled with agent are the safest and easiest component of the arsenal, since the containers are not married to propellant, they became the focus of the next campaign. Burning one-ton containers was a way to catch up, so that at the end of the incinerator's first year, PR literature could boast that a substantial portion of the stockpile was destroyed. But the ton container campaign also ran aground when Trina Allen blew the whistle on them for burning Lewisite. With two strikes and no balls, they moved on to a campaign to destroy agent-filled bombs.

Meanwhile, there were lots of other calamities. The plant was shut down by a power failure. Agent "migration" was detected in observation corridors and dangerous decontamination fluid seeped through cracks in a concrete floor. There were computer malfunctions and problems with slag build up in the pollution abatement system. The Utah Department of Environmental Quality cited the plant operator for twenty-five violations, including "numerous instances of noncompliance." Vials of agent were misplaced and lost. A group of Kentuckians on a PR tour of the facility were inadvertently exposed to a nerve agent contaminated artillery shell but not notified until an anonymous source called and told them. When a worker forgot to replace a washer on a bolt, 140 gallons of agent spilled inside the plant. Miraculously, no one died.

The bad acts at the Utah burner were reruns of those at the JACADS pilot plant in the South Pacific. JACADS had a major leak in its first year. Later, an M-55 rocket blew up inside a furnace and punched a hole in its wall. Another time it was shut down by a fire. Then another M-55 exploded while being processed. The EPA fined JACADS for failing to deal with its hazardous waste properly. A 700-pound bomb leaked its contents on to the floor. A worker was decapitated when a section of a feed shoot fell on him. There were so many delays and cost overruns that the permit ran out and had to be renewed. The crises at JACADS modeled those that would be repeated in Utah. TOCDF, after all, was nothing more than JACADS' fat younger twin.

TOCDF's troubles were not just glitches. Major components of the incineration system fell apart. The dunage furnace for burning packing waste never worked. The Brine Reduction Area, a means of dealing with the voluminous brine byproducts of incineration, had so many problems that they eventually gave up on it, too. The collapse of these two legs of the incinerator design means that for every pound of chemical agent burned, fifteen pounds of hazardous waste is produced. Consequently, in the first year and a half of its operation, TOCDF produced more than 45 million pounds of ash, brine, laboratory waste, metals, and other pollution that had to be shipped to hazardous waste facilities in Texas, Tennessee, California, Colorado, Illinois, and Idaho. And, of course, to Utah's West Desert environmental sacrifice zone. Some of the toxic stuff was buried, some was burned again, and some was injected into deep wells. Some of the dumps it went to are in minority and poor communities. Our tax dollars made it happen.

Alternatives to incineration are criticized by incinerator proponents for making too much back-end waste. As it became apparent that TOCDF's waste stream is so inflated, it also became clear that alternatives are cleaner and more efficient because incineration has not lived up to inflated claims and expectations. Meanwhile, as we wait for better solutions, TOCDF's toxic legacy is spreading downwind and downstream all around America.

Some of that toxic legacy may be coming straight out the incinerator smokestacks. In its first year and a half of operation, there were at least forty-two "stack alarms," meaning that monitors designed to detect agent in the smokestack set off alarms. Over and over, EG&G, the army, and state regulators denied that it was agent setting off the alarms. But Tim Thomas, the army project manager, testified under oath that there had been at least six confirmed agent stack alarms, and that was way back in March of '97.

At the end of March of 1998, at the beginning of the bomb campaign, a major leak of agent into the Utah air occurred, according to a team of independent experts hired by CWWG to analyze the evidence. After Sarin nerve agent was drained from a bomb so it could be fed into the liquid incinerator, the bomb was "probed" to see if any agent remained. Apparently, workers were having a hard time getting the probe instrument in and out of the bomb to get an accurate reading. At some point they either gave up and sent the bomb to a metal parts furnace or mistakenly thought the bomb was empty. Either way, they were wrong. A bomb, still filled with about seventy-five pounds of nerve agent went into the metal parts furnace. Agent burns hot like fuel. The presence of so much agent in the metal parts furnace sent the temperature up and into the danger zone. An emergency shutdown of the furnace was triggered.

What happened to the agent? Was it burned up as incinerator operators claim, or did it go out the stack and downwind as critics charge? Unfortunately, the monitoring and alarm systems that could provide some insight were temporarily turned off. The required staggering of alarms in the stack to detect agent was not happening at the time. After the incident, the "backup tubes" designed to confirm agent presence were pulled and thrown into a box with about thirty other tubes, unlabeled and unidentifiable for confirmation of a leak. Although the only alarm that was working "buried the needle" in the red, indicating that at least five hundred times the allowable limit was released into the open air, the army claims it wasn't agent that caused the alarm. State regulators agreed. Documents obtained by CWWG lawyers, however, indicate that the army and EG&G were desperate to know all they could about weather conditions and wind patterns the day after, behavior that reveals a concern that nerve agent did get loose in the air.

Lawyers for the CWWG took what available data there was and turned it over to outside experts to examine the evidence. They concluded that agent went out the stack, perhaps as much as seventy pounds, about three times the amount that drifted over Skull Valley during the infamous sheep kill of 1968. Utah has moved from an era of duck'n'cover to an era of leak'n'cover. The bottom line remained the same — Utahns were still downwind from reckless military incompetence.

What if agent went out the open stack of the Utah incinerator and dispersed? No one dropped dead downwind, not even a sheep. Does that mean no one encountered the agent and no harm was done? Ask Gulf War vets those questions and they can fill up the rest of your day with grim and heart-breaking stories, all with one underlining theme: we do not know what health impacts nerve agent has had at low doses. In fact, according to Government Accounting Office and National Research Council reports released in 1998, we have little reliable information about nerve agent toxicity. Nerve agent may be toxic at much lower levels than assumed. Unfortunately, the military has no plans to find out more.

In the winter of 1997, the people of Utah got a strong dose of the anecdotal evidence that a little nerve gas goes a long way. James Tuite, the charismatic and brilliant Senate investigator who brought the question of nerve agent exposure and Gulf War illness before Congress, came to town for a symposium with Paul Sullivan, an articulate organizer of Gulf War vets. Dr Howard Urnovitz of the Chronic Illness Research Foundation also accompanied them. They were sponsored by Families Against Incinerator Risk.

FAIR was started by Lisa Puchner with the help of her friends, Kim and Ken Smith. An aspiring filmmaker who made a documentary about Utah's atomic downwinders, she had lived in southern Utah while interviewing the Bullock family of ranchers and was moved by their stories of suffering and appalled by the military's reckless disregard for public health. When she moved back to Salt Lake from St George, she was alarmed to find that the conditions were in play for a new generation of downwinders, which included her own children. Today FAIR is run by Jason Groenewold, a very talented and able young organizer, and has more than a thousand members. Lisa and I sit on the FAIR board together.

The Gulf War Symposium at Westminster College followed a number of teach-ins there that were organized by FAIR to raise consciousness and gather members. Cindy King, Steve

Jones, and I had conducted the teach-ins and acted as advisors. The symposium and a preceding press conference would announce FAIR's presence loud and clear. Craig Williams of the CWWG also flew in to speak. More than three hundred people braved a snowstorm on a February morning to attend and most stayed the day, fascinated by the compelling case that was laid out before them.

After their one-sided triumph in the Gulf, more than a hundred thousand soldiers returned home and took up their lives and careers where they had left off when the call to war came. Unlike our Vietnam vets, Gulf War vets suffered little ambiguity about their accomplishments. They fought a despicable bad guy and had overwhelming popular backing. They won hands down. And, incredibly, they suffered barely a scratch. Or, at least, they thought that was the case.

In the months that followed, strange symptoms began to appear. There were rashes, diarrhea, memory loss, confusion, and headaches. As time went by, rare cancers and chronic illnesses also appeared. Babies were born with serious disabilities. Men and women who had been fit and robust were crippled by debilitating diseases that seemed to fit no known pattern. A few at a time, they found one another and tried to understand what they had in common. What they had in common, they soon realized, was exposure to nerve gas.

The stories that emerged from the ranks of the Gulf War vets told of bunkers of Iraqi chemical weapons that were openly detonated. Winds that circled the Persian Gulf landscape recycled the gas far and wide. There were accounts of nerve gas alarms going off and confusion about their reliability and meaning. And, of course, there were stories about exposure to radiation from the new "depleted uranium" artillery shells that so cleanly pierced the Iraqi's Soviet tanks. Oil-well fires and pesticides to keep down the desert's biting insects also added to the toxic brew. During the lunch break, ailing members of the Dugway Workers' League shared notes with the Gulf vets and discovered they also shared a common set of shots from military doctors who assured them they knew what they were doing.

Tuite and Sullivan described the pathways of exposure, the investigation and ongoing cover-ups. Dr Urnovitz explained the synergistic potential of vaccines and pollution to cripple health and the mysteries of toxicity that we were only beginning to understand. He explained that although the government is required to oversee risk assessments to calculate the hazards of proposed polluting projects, we really have no way of analyzing nervous system, reproductive, and immune system risk. Science also has no way to evaluate the synergistic effects of exposure to several chemicals at once. The EPA has confirmed that the combined effects of two pesticides encountered together can be a thousand times more potent than the impact of each encountered alone, but the typical risk assessment keeps each pollutant in its own analytical box. Likewise, no connection is assumed between viruses and pollution, although an immune system compromised by exposure to pollution may provide a pathway for an opportunistic virus that would normally be resisted. No, officially and formally, we take a narrow linear look at cancer risk alone and ignore other aspects of our health until obvious damage can be shown. This "dead body" approach to risk assessment makes guinea pigs out of downwinders.

Even the limited risk assessments we do require can be bogus. The risk assessment for TOCDF does not look at the dangers to nursing downwind infants, despite a typically Mormon high birthrate that guarantees lots of nursing infants. That population group is usually included in health risk assessments because they are especially vulnerable to endocrine disruptors that may bioaccumulate in the fat of their mothers' milk and be passed into their fragile developing systems. The study also denies that Tooele County residents, again typical Mormons, grow lots of their own food, "put it by," and consume it. We have a thousand backyard orchards and gardens plus four meatpacking plants that just cut local beef for local consumption. Incredibly, the scenario that they chose to measure our health risk is based on a subsistence prawn farmer who eats his own product. Many of my neighbors could not tell you what a prawn is. Nevertheless, the state assures them that the risks of incineration are acceptable based on that contrived scenario.

Craig Williams dissected the troubled chem demil program, relentlessly laying bare its lies and failures. He sounded a clear warning that chemical weapons incineration in Tooele County could expose the populous Wasatch Front to nerve agent when the inevitable leak occurred. Steve Jones explained how to calculate "kill zones" for nerve gas. Take out a map and draw a line forty miles long in any direction from the TOCDF burner, he said, and anyone along that path could die. That night, Tuite, Sullivan, and I appeared on television to warn that "Gulf War illness could be coming to a neighborhood near you."

Since that snowy afternoon in '97, national Gulf War vets organizations have gone on record repeatedly to condemn incineration and support the search for alternatives. They learned the hard way, long before the GAO and NRC chimed in, that even trace amounts of agent are dangerous. They know the costs of exposure personally. They are more than familiar with how the military lies and covers its tracks, refuses to be accountable, and puts its victims on the defensive.

The alliance between military veterans, the civilian walking wounded of the Cold War, and those who refuse to be the next victims is a natural and powerful one. The Vietnam Veterans of America Foundation has also been a reliable ally in the struggle to replace chemical weapons incineration with a safe and clean alternative technology. Vietnam vets have prior experience with dioxins. Thousands of them were exposed to Agent Orange when the war was extended to the foliage and ecosystem of Vietnam. Dioxins are in Agent Orange and now they are in Vietnam vets. More than twenty years after the war, they also show up in Vietnamese mothers and their children. Cancer, cover-up, chronic illness and birth defects—they have lived the story that is old now. Like the West Desert HEAL volunteers, vets also know that epidemiologists wield imprecise tools and that an unbiased expert is hard to find. They know that whether the subject is the consequences of Agent Orange or the impact of low-level nerve gas exposure, one study will confirm their own analysis of their ills and the next study will shoot it down. Systems that are synergistic, complex, and dynamic, from the human body to the ecobody, are hard to sort out in the conventional arenas for defining risk and deciding liability.

Craig Williams is a Vietnam veteran who leads the CWWG's struggle against incineration in favor of alternatives out of the Kentucky Environmental Foundation offices in Berea, Kentucky. He is a bright charismatic leader, a loud and gruff sounding New York transplant who lightens his passionate and outraged attack on the chem demil program with liberal doses of sharp wit and self-deprecating humor. Craig earned his suspicion of military programs the hard way. He did a tour in Vietnam where, as an interpreter, he saw the dark side of the US military and learned how torturers and others of their ilk who know their deeds will surely be condemned must lie to stay in business. Williams returned angry and disillusioned. He helped organize opposition to the war among Vietnam vets and eventually helped found the Vietnam Veterans of America. Then, like many of the refugees from the personal and social turmoil of the sixties, he retreated to the background. Unlike the expatriates of an earlier era who fled to Paris and Barcelona, the expatriates of the seventies escaped to rural America. Craig landed in Berea where he started a family, became a cabinetmaker, and coached Little League baseball. He'd had enough of political struggle. He planned to settle down.

That all changed in 1984 when three hundred or so citizens gathered to hear about the army's plan to incinerate the stockpile of nerve gas weapons at the Bluegrass Army Depot in Lexington. The citizens who lived near Bluegrass, like citizens near any military facility, had firsthand experience with the lack of competence and responsibility that characterized Cold War military activity. In what became known as the "smokepot incident" in 1979, Bluegrass sent a toxic cloud over I-75 that sent forty people to the hospital with respiratory problems and then denied it for two weeks. Five years later, as the military spokesman tried to explain their plans and field questions from concerned citizens, it was clear, he recalls, they didn't know what they were doing and didn't care much what citizens thought about it. The chem demil program was born without civilian witnesses and had no checks or balances. The Cold Warriors who managed our chemical weapons were a secretive lot who had never made an inclusive decision in their careers. The crowd that day was a baffling experience for them. Here we go again, thought Williams.

At home, his wife implored him to use the skills she knew he had to create an opposition to the army's half-baked plans. Their children were at stake. In 1986, a local Kentucky opposition group, Common Ground, took shape. Common Ground founded the Kentucky Environmental Foundation, or KEF, after more than two thousand local citizens packed a "scoping" meeting for the program that was held in a middle school near the planned incinerator. Craig was hired to lead KEF.

Also in 1990, the army brought citizens together from stockpile communities to a conference in Lexington that many of the citizen participants found to be a big dog and pony show for incineration. They wandered out and found a restaurant where they could caucus. They decided that it would be wise to break out of their isolation and continue the dialogue they had begun. So, in 1991, with the support of Greenpeace, the Military Toxics Project, and the Tides Foundation, KEF organized the first "Citizen's Summit" on chemical weapons disposal in Richmond, Kentucky. That was the year they moved beyond a "not in my backyard" perspective that favored shipping it all to Utah to a more inclusive, unified, and broad-looking approach. The "Citizen's Accords" were written and the Chemical Weapons Working Group became an umbrella for the broad range of grass roots groups springing up in the stockpile communities, the proposed sites for eight massive incinerators.

Craig came to Utah the following spring and visited Janet Cook's home with Steve Erickson and Cindy King. Sandy Covello and I drove over there to meet him. I attended the second Citizen's Summit later that spring. By then, Craig was surrounded by a small but impressive staff. Elizabeth Crowe was a bright, independent, and thoroughly competent young woman who had hung on to the high ideals that she began to practice in college. Melissa Tuckey was a natural-born organizer who had learned to be both persuasive and tenacious while organizing for labor and canvassing door to door in Ohio. John Capillo had been a priest in Brooklyn for fourteen years and had worked among the poor in war-torn El Salvador. Later, Lois Kleffman's wise countenance would be added to the staff. The delegates from across the nation knew a good thing when they saw it. During the second Citizen's Summit, KEF was elected to lead the CWWG.

I returned from that conference impressed but unsure. True to my library calling, I researched the issues I heard raised. I found lots of breakfast cereal for two-headed babies rhetoric that was hard to sort out. The engineering information was challenging. I am not a mechanical guy. Stick me in coveralls and drop me in any garage in the morning and I will be fired by noon. But common sense tells me a technological process that generates thousands of degrees of heat and is concluded with an open stack to the atmosphere is more likely to have an accident that emits downwind than one that operates at low temperature and is designed as a closed loop. That is particularly important when you add nerve agent into the equation. They were not roasting pigs out there at TOCDF. From the start, CWWG delegates have insisted that the bottom-line criterion for an "alternative" disposal technology had to be its ability to contain its byproducts during both normal and upset conditions.

Then it occurred to me: my family and neighbors and I would resolve the pro and con arguments over incineration with our own flesh and blood. If you come back in twenty years and look at our cancer rates, our clusters of chronic illnesses, our infant mortality, and the twisted bodies of our children whose genes were bent in the womb, then you may be able to conclude which side was right. No one disputes whether atomic radiation is harmful or harmless as they did in the fifties because atomic downwinders wrote the answer on their deathbeds. We would be the test subjects in this next military-industrial experiment.

It is important that citizens have power over the technologies that land in their communities and could land in their blood. Citizen power over technology should not be limited to the means to monitor. Real power is not just voice but choice. My decision to oppose the chem demil juggernaut that spring had a larger context than TOCDF in Utah. I also wanted to help people in Alabama, Oregon, Arkansas, Colorado, Kentucky, Maryland, and Indiana who wanted choice, not just voice.

I also concluded that in Utah, even voice was missing. I believed the popular notion that when you give government, especially big government, a blank check and look the other way, they tend to screw up. Chem demil is a good example. It was designed during the military's blank check era. Government performs better if it is watched closely, questioned, and challenged. It struck me as odd that county commissioners who worried about their "right" to graze cattle on public land assumed the Bureau of Land Management should be watched but were easy about giving the army a green light to burn chemical weapons. When was the last time a cow blew up and went downwind? Aren't health and safety also rights?

The genius of the American political system is checks and balances. When citizens don't pay attention and show up, a critical check is lost. TOCDF's vocal critics in Utah could be counted on one hand. In Tooele County, the actual site of CAMDS and TOCDF, you could count them by putting your hands behind your back. I decided to play a role in my community because no one else was playing it. Every town needs its Boy Scout leaders and basketball coaches, but it also needs a town crier. I was well suited for the job. I knew the military's numerous local boosters would label me a crank but I seemed to have an unlimited capacity for embarrassment. I also understood that the integrity and quality of the ecobody, the health and wellbeing of my own body, and the vigor of democratic practices within the political culture are intimately linked. They feedback one another in a dynamic mix. Think of it as the ecology of risk and the keystone species is the citizen activist. I was often asked by exasperated incinerator proponents, "what if everyone thought like you?" It seemed to me that the question missed the point. I was certain the day would never come when everyone thought like me. But what if my voice was missing? Who would replace my voice in the dialogue?

I consulted my family and they were supportive. Activism would be more of a shift in focus than a new pac   /hen our kids were little we were always running after them and picking up. Then Linda went back to college so she could teach and I did a busy stint as Mr Mom. Then I went to grad school. By the time I finished, she was busy attending to the troubled families of children she taught. One day she'd be getting the Lion's Club to buy eyeglasses for a child whose family couldn't afford them and the next day she was arranging free plastic surgery for a boy who was born with one ear. Our habit of compulsive over-commitment, from grad school to charity, was well established. Still, meetings require time away from family and phone calls intrude on home life. In the final analysis, I justified the sacrifices I would make at home to play the role of activist in the community as a mature expression of parenting. Kids grow up and go out in the world. Mine were already reaching for the door. The circle of parental concern was expanding to include a wider world where getting a summer job at the depot laundry and being exposed to work clothes soaked with solvent could result in a weakened immune system and reproductive problems, as one neighbor learned the hard way. I could see just far enough around the next curve in my life to wish for healthy grandchildren. By the next conference, I was an active and committed member.

CWWG annual conferences realize high expectations every year. Delegates face a packed and demanding agenda. They work hard. One year we cobbled together a white paper on technological alternatives to incineration called the "Citizen's Solution" while also setting a coordinated strategy for the coming year to stall incineration and get funding for alternatives. We did it in three days. I did a lot of the writing. Imagine the patience and perseverance that is required to sit still while forty people cross Ts and dot Is, literally. It was an adventure in consensus editing.

The history of the CWWG annual conferences also offers testimony to the will of delegates to stay in the room through mentally and emotionally draining sessions to reach common goals. Each year, after pulling together the next year's strategy, the conference concludes in a press conference, scripted and rehearsed collectively the night before. Sleep-starved and talked-out delegates stand up, hold hands, and speak out in unison before dispersing across Capitol Hill to lobby. The press who cover these events and the Congressional aids who receive the participants afterward probably don't know it, but they are looking at a little miracle.

The CWWG practices a kind of consensus democracy that requires loads of talking, explaining, debating, and sharing among its practitioners. Delegates have the opportunity to bond with others who share their values, visions, and commitment. But they must also navigate the treacherous white water of factional debate, where the jagged edges of powerful egos hide just under the surface of discourse. When you put forty bright and dynamic people who are also assertive and passionate in a room together for ten hours a day, three days running, careful steering is required to get through the debating and hit the targets. In my day-job career, I spend much time with library boards, city councils, and county commissions. I am accustomed to watching strong and opinionated personalities contend with one another. But until I attended a CWWG conference, I never encountered so many people in one place who routinely stand up to speak and start with "I have three points—first of all …" By evening, I experienced a kind of verbal burnout that made silence seem like a precious salve. I have found myself following intense CWWG discussions and thinking, "this is why people buy dogs—they don't talk."

Consensus is also challenged by diversity. The CWWG

includes native Hawaiians who are exposing and opposing the troubled JACADS burner in their backyard and Utahns who now have two incinerators, CAMDS and TOCDF, in their backyard. From Alabama, Arkansas, and Kentucky come a mix of races and classes. Oregon's delegates include Native American tribal leaders from Umatilla. Each year, Russian delegates from sick and dying stockpile and production site communities over there attend and share. Differences that could divide do not, because delegates understand that dioxins do not discriminate.

Delegates play hard, too. They go out to dinner together, close down bars, and then cluster in hotel rooms to laugh and tell stories. I think people who view our activism from afar see mostly the grim issues we face and the gritty work we do. They only glimpse the pleasure of friendship and alliance among people who share purpose and compelling themes, like safeguarding the health of loved ones. When navigating rough water, respect and affection make good oars.

Coordinated grassroots organizing and activism has provided a platform for other means of opposition. In July of '96, lawyers for the CWWG, the Sierra Club, and the Vietnam Veterans of America Foundation took the army, EG&G, and the State of Utah to court for endangering downwinders and violating environmental law. A preliminary injunction hearing was held before Judge Tina Campbell to determine whether TOCDF should be shut down until a trial could be held. The burden of proof is especially tough in preliminary injunction hearings and the judge said no and allowed TOCDF to keep burning. Later that year, lawyers also failed to persuade Utah's Hazardous

Waste Board to shut it down. Another preliminary injunction hearing was held in March of '97. Again, the burning was allowed to continue. In 1996, Westinghouse won a $575 million-dollar contract to build an incinerator in Anniston, Alabama. In 1997, Raytheon Corporation, the builder and operator of the troubled JACADS facility, was awarded contracts to build incinerators in Pine Bluff, Arkansas, and Umatilla, Oregon. Legal actions to challenge permits in Arkansas, Alabama, and Oregon are underway. In December of 1998, a judge in Oregon questioned that state's permit decisions so far and sent regulators back for better information on nerve agent toxicity.

Although the struggle in the legal arena has been frustrating, it has also been strategically successful because it has supported a vigorous challenge in the halls of Congress. During Utah's courthouse sessions I often counted as many as a dozen suits on the other side. Our legal team was primarily Mick Harrison, Richard Condit, Robert Ukeiley, Ashley Schanauer, and Robert Guild. We were clearly outgunned and losing. Or were we? The legal arena generated voluminous amounts of damning documents, like diaries, reports, letters, and memos. It let incineration opponents over the wall to gather evidence that was valuable when making a case to Congress to stop incineration and fund alternatives. Over and over, our devoted attorneys showed that the face chem demil presented to Congress and the public contrasted sharply with the countenance it assumed when it thought it was hidden behind locked gates. Internal communication exudes fear, doubt, conflict, incompetence, and cover-up that contradict the confident demeanor shown outwardly. It is a disturbing picture and Congress has now seen it thanks to the legal team's selfless efforts. The fate of the program lies, ultimately, with Congress. Congress gives the program its budget and marching orders.

In 1996, proposed Maryland and Indiana incinerators were dropped in favor of chemical neutralization, a closed-loop or non-smokestack disposal method that can contain releases of nerve agent under upset conditions. The following year, planned incinerators for Kentucky and Colorado were put on hold until at least two alternative disposal technologies were tested for development. ACWA was, in no small measure, also a result of persistent legal challenges by our team of dogged and savvy investigators.

The search for an escape route from the failures and risks of chemical weapons incineration is known as the Assembled Chemical Weapons Assessment, or ACWA, Dialogue. It is a key to the chemical weapons demilitarization process because it provides the public with a specific vision of what is possible once the incineration dinosaur is abandoned. The alternative technologies, like "plasma arc conversion" and "super critical water oxidation," that are being tested and developed under ACWA may offer marketable solutions to a wide range of hazardous waste problems around the world. In marked contrast to the incineration program, citizens were given a prominent place at the ACWA power table early on when the all-important criteria were set for future decision making about alternative technology development.

The more open and inclusive ACWA Dialogue has not precluded PMCD from trying to manipulate and compromise the process whenever it can. In the summer of 1999, Craig Williams charged that PMCD chief Ted Prociv ensured a technology vendor challenge to the ACWA procurement process and subsequent critical delays in the testing schedule when he only made enough money available for testing three of the six alternative technologies that satisfied the criteria set by Dialogue members. Prociv claimed he just couldn't find any more dollars for testing, but Williams charged he was sitting on at least 200 million of them. The accounting practices that allowed Prociv to stonewall ACWA participants, Congress, and the media were described by auditors as "Mexican banking" that was "almost criminal." At least one senator privately fumed he had been lied to.

Still, the Dialogue stands in startling contrast to the usual case where citizens can't show up until they're asked to "comment" on decisions that are already made and deals that are already cut. The change is a fitting tribute to the credibility and political power CWWG delegates have achieved together. It provides real-world evidence of the CWWG slogan I wrote, "When concerned citizens are empowered, creative solutions will follow."

Maryland and Indiana dodged the incinerator bullet, at least in part, because the stockpiles there consisted only of one-ton containers that were obviously easier to treat with neutralization than the diverse collections of hard-shelled munitions in the other stockpiles. But another reason those proposed incinerators and those in Kentucky and Colorado were abandoned is because legislators in those states passed legislation making the permit requirements for incinerators so tough that the chem demil gang knew they couldn't meet them. There is a consensus among program watchers that Kentucky, in particular, will never go to an incinerator. The public there is aware, interested, and well organized. Their CAC has been loaded with activists. Their Congressional delegation responds accordingly. So although the CWWG case provides dramatic evidence of the importance of national organizing and cooperation, the local political component is also key.

Utah has two chemical weapons incinerators because the state's politicians are wary of, if not hostile to, environmental regulation. Their bias shows up in state regulatory agencies that have given the army and its contractor a free ride. When asked by worried Utahns why their Department of Environmental Quality has "failed," I reply that it hasn't. Utah's DEQ is the perfect political expression of the governor who appoints its director and the legislature that sets its budget and gives its marching orders. While Kentucky legislative leaders from both parties stand together on their capitol's steps and refuse incineration, Utah's legislators have remained silent. While both houses of Georgia's legislature voted unanimously to ask the federal government to hold hearings in Georgia on Alabama's proposed incinerator, the Republican majority leader of the Utah State Senate was calling in to a radio talkshow to berate me for being an "obstructionist." The lack of a viable two-party political system in Utah, where Democrats are overwhelmingly outnumbered, is in itself an impediment to the kind of political debate that can illuminate the issues raised by the incineration controversy. Finally, Utahns face incineration today because we are uncomfortable challenging authority and we are self-conscious about our patriotism. As long as the military sees patriotic trust as an invitation to site dangerous snake oil projects they can't put anywhere else, Utah is vulnerable. Can it be coincidental that we got atomic testing, Dugway, half the chemical weapons and two incinerators?

As the "incineration trial" in federal court unfolded in June of 1999, it became clear that worker exposure to nerve agent was becoming common. Even when nerve agent readings are taken from the bare skin of workers who are cut out of their protective butyl suits, the army refuses to consider them exposed. Sadly, a new generation of workers will suffer the fate of Dugway workers. TOCDF went into a "voluntary stand-down" during the two weeks that lawyers Mick Harrison and Richard Condit relentlessly peeled the program down to reveal its reckless failures, perhaps to insure that further embarrassing incidents would not occur while they were at it.

Testimony about the 30 March 1998 emergency shutdown of the metal parts incinerator was particularly revealing. Although the furnace, loaded with an improperly drained bomb casing with more than seventy pounds of nerve agent in it, got so hot it shutdown and triggered nerve agent alarms in a vent between it and the smokestack, alarms in the smokestack itself did not go off. Later testing of the device showed it was "saturated" with a "nerve agent-like chemical" that plant managers could not identify, but insisted was not nerve agent. The worker who monitored the alarm in question was told not to treat the all-important sample tubes from the device as "alarm" samples, despite the fact that the plant's personnel were running around in gas masks trying to figure out what went wrong. Instead, the worker tossed the unmarked sample tubes into a box of other unlabeled tubes. Deliberate deception or another case of "Hey, Mo!"? The judge will rule sometime in the fall.

When the trial concluded, CWWG's student interns and citizen volunteers carted and loaded boxes of evidence into a station wagon with a duct taped window and broken gate latch parked in front of the federal building on Main Street in Salt Lake. The documents in the cartons would supply the ammunition for another CWWG assault on incineration in the halls of Congress. Nearby, public relations consultants were hastily arranging lawyers for the army and EG&G behind microphones and spinning the local press their version of events. As Harrison and Condit drove off into the sunset, the US army stood on the courthouse steps, smiled at the cameras, and covered its ass.

NINE

STORMING THE CASTLE
OF THE INVISIBLE ECOTHUG

"The bees are out." That's the expression workers at Magcorp use to describe their work environment when there is so much chlorine gas in the air that skin turns lobster red and stings. Magcorp is a magnesium refinery on the southwest arm of the Great Salt Lake, on the rim of the West Desert. Each year its corroded smokestacks pump about 60 million pounds of chlorine gas and about 6 million pounds of hydrochloric acid into the open air. It is the single source for about 85 percent of all "point source" chlorine gas emissions in the US and also the top polluter for hydrochloric acid, making Magcorp the dirtiest industrial operation in America.

Magcorp's remote desert location on the uninhabited west side of the Great Salt Lake leaves it out of sight and out of mind. Weekend sailors on the Great Salt Lake may have experienced an occasional unpleasant encounter with Magcorp's pollution, but most people couldn't locate it on a map. Even in Grantsville, the nearest town, Magcorp was usually a distant plume. Exposure is episodic. I had lived in Grantsville for many months before I was aware of it. The wind has to be blowing just so to carry the plume down and through town so that the bleach-like odor is obvious and sometimes dramatic. Once we became aware, however, a faint whiff of chlorine was often noticeable when the weather moved from north to south.

As time went by, I became more familiar with Magcorp's stench. Chlorine is extremely corrosive and the liner of their unique pollution control device, the chlorine reduction burner, or CRB, wears out every few years. While it is being replaced, Magcorp operates with no pollution control whatsoever for months at a time. Grantsville then lives under a caustic smudge. This is also true during the weather inversions that are common to mountainous landscapes in winter. High levels of chlorine gas can cause severe pulmonary damage and even kill when experienced up close and personal. It was, after all, used as a chemical weapon in World War One. But there is little definitive research about the health impacts of low exposure over time. Local regulators tell us that what they don't know can't hurt us. The state has also reassured residents that only low harmless doses are reaching them, but my family knows firsthand how sensitivity to chlorine grows. What was once just an annoying odor now causes severe headaches. People with sinus problems and asthma, especially children, stay inside or bear the unpleasant consequences when Magcorp is in our air and up our noses.

A neighbor who cuts hair for a living said she always knows when a customer works at Magcorp because his hair is "so brittle and weird." Workers park their cars next to the Grantsville cemetery and ride company buses out to the refinery because the caustic and corrosive air out there eats the finish off their cars. Magcorp workers are "well paid" and like to buy shiny double-cab pick-ups that are powerful enough to pull boats, or trailers loaded with the dirt bikes, ATVs, and snowmobiles that are the material reward for working in an environment usually described as "Hell." It doesn't make sense to ruin the rewards of your sacrifice by parking them too close to the sacrifice zone.

Although it is common knowledge that Magcorp's pollution eats paint off metal and brittles human hair, no one has ever looked at what it does to the lungs of the five hundred plus people who work there. Or what it does to the five million plus migrating birds who nest and feed along the shores of Great Salt Lake under toxic air. Or, until quite recently, whether burning massive volumes of chlorine produces dioxins. In a climate of scarcity, industrial revenues and high-paying jobs take priority over questions about potential health problems. As one neighbor put it, "smells like jobs to me." In such an atmosphere, the forecast is for days of denial, excuse, and exception.

Not everyone can stand to work in the foul green air under a yellow plume. Over the years I have lived in Grantsville, I have met many people who tried and only lasted a week or two before they quit. They describe a factory that resembles a sprawling junkyard car, wired together and covered in rich red rust. Flammable, acidic, and explosive chemicals are encountered at every turn. Magcorp is Utah Power and Light's number one customer because their manufacturing process is electrolitic. Imagine, they say, all that heavy electrical current pouring through a corroded factory full of dangerous and volatile chemicals within a pall of poisonous pollution. Hell on Earth, indeed.

We have to take their word for it. You cannot visit Magcorp on your own. It is several miles off the beaten track, in this case

I-80, forty miles west of Salt Lake City. It stands alone on the desert horizon. If you should go out of your way to find it, there are gates and guards with strict orders and tough demeanors. The guards get their orders from Magcorp's corporate officers who don't talk to the press and certainly don't talk to critics. They barely talk to federal and state agencies who supposedly have the authority to monitor and regulate their operation. The officers, in turn, take their lack-of-communication cue from Ira Rennert, the man who owns Magcorp lock, stock, and dirty barrel.

Rennert is a reclusive mega-millionaire who has spent his long financial career flying low to avoid the radar of reporters, investors, regulators, or anyone else who might ask embarrassing questions or demand accountability. When I was first researching Rennert and his company, Renco, for a group of concerned citizens who wondered who actually owned that stinking factory in our backyard, I could find no clippings, photos, or references on the Internet. I had never encountered a corporation that produced no promotional brochures, news releases, or even a plain fact sheet. I couldn't locate an annual report. This was unusual for a corporation that employed as many as 10,500 workers and was ranked by *Forbes* in 1997 as fifty-first among the nation's top private companies. All I learned was that Magcorp was owned by Renco, Renco had 2.5 billion dollars in annual income, and that some guy named Ira Rennert was the head honcho.

In 1995, Rennert and Renco briefly hit the headlines when Renco's executive vice-president, Marvin Koenig, was accused of luring a young woman up to the company's forty-second floor offices in Rockefeller Plaza and then raping her at knifepoint on a conference-room table. Koenig ended up settling out of court for an undisclosed sum of money. He bargained a guilty plea down to sexual misconduct and got three years' probation. Amazingly, he went right on working for Renco. Rennert slipped back into the shadows. Although little information was available on Rennert, it seemed clear he was a man who kept his own counsel, cared little for the opinion of others, and knew how to use a loophole when he found one.

Driving through loopholes in regulations is a pattern that Utahns know well. The corporate officers of Magcorp could write the book. First of all, Magcorp avoids rules because it is a one-of-a-kind operation in the United States, probably because its raw material for magnesium is also unique. The Great Salt Lake, true to its name, is a huge reservoir of salts and other minerals. Once part of a larger inland sea, Lake Bonneville, Great Salt Lake is at once a concentrated legacy of the minerals from that larger body of water and a basin with no outlet for all the minerals that wash down from surrounding mountains. Magcorp leases about 100,000 acres of Bureau of Land Management ground, much of it now contaminated with industrial waste, for evaporation ponds that collect lake water loaded with magnesium chloride that is left when the water evaporates. Electricity is used to split the magnesium chloride and separate out the magnesium. For every pound of magnesium thus produced, three pounds of free chlorine also results. To get rid of it, Magcorp has a "chlorine reduction burner," its main pollution control device. No other industry has one because no one else is dealing with that electrolitic manufacturing process.

Regulators set rules first for those activities that are common and multistate in nature. As the EPA sets standards and outlines expectations for various kinds of pollution beyond those common "criteria pollutants" that were the early focus of our clean air legislation, it determines something called a MACT, or "maximum achievable control technology." Typically, it looks at all those manufacturers who produce the kind of pollution in question. It identifies which of those industrial operations are doing the best job at controlling that kind of emission and then sets a MACT standard that reflects the best controls it identifies. Magcorp's lawyers argue that, since they are a "one'n'only" operation, whatever they are currently doing must be the "best." Who, they ask, is doing better? There is a similar refinery in Norway that does a far better job of controlling its well-documented pollution, but foreign plants are rarely considered. Normally, only domestic operations count when the EPA looks for a MACT.

Many of the regulations and policies that might apply to Magcorp are toothless because Magcorp was "grandfathered in" when new clean air rules were applied to old operations. At the time, Utah state and local governments were far more concerned with how all those fancy new federal clean air rules would impact a money maker like Magcorp than the air quality they were designed to improve. Again, jobs and revenue were seen as a fair trade for environmental quality. Finally, state and federal regulators tend to focus their limited resources and staff on those problems that are brought to their attention. The squeaky wheel, as they say, gets the grease. In the absence of any local political pressure to make sure Magcorp is in compliance, the state's Department of Environmental Quality did minimum and often superficial enforcement.

*

In June of 1996, a small group of Utah's environmental activists came together to make a difference. The time had come to ask why so little was required from the source for 90 percent of Utah's toxic pollution. The notion to go after Magcorp originated in the first biennial Great Salt Lake Issues Forum, organized by the Friends of Great Salt Lake to address a wide range of challenges to the integrity of a unique and barely understood ecosystem that harbored millions of migrating birds each season. Those who followed up at a meeting in a back room at the Southern Utah Wilderness Alliance offices included leaders from FOGSL, SUWA, the Sierra Club, West Desert HEAL, the Wasatch Clean Air Coalition, and the Audubon Society. In subsequent meetings we distilled into a core group that included myself, Howard Gross, Scott Endicott, and Erin Moore.

Howard was, like me, a native of New Jersey who was also enthralled by the physical beauty of the Western landscapes he encountered. Trained as an ecologist, he did environmental consulting and was more than familiar with the regulatory buttons that could be pushed and how to do so. In 1999, he became the director of Hawkwatch, an organization that uses the health of predatory birds to measure the integrity and health of desert ecosystems. Scott was a brilliant biochemist working for the University of Utah and a leader of the Utah Sierra Club. Erin was a paid staff member of SUWA. Her diminutive stature belied the strength, dynamic energy, and determination she brought to any environmental issue she decided to address. Around the core was a talented pool of lawyers like Joro Walker, scientists like Ty Harrison and Ric Cuchetto, and activists like Ivan Weber, Nina Dougherty, and Lynn deFreitas. Another core group member preferred to stay anonymous and was referred to by the others as "Deep Throat." He had been employed at Magcorp years ago and, based on firsthand experience of its belligerent and paranoid corporate culture, feared he could be sued for his participation even though he divulged no manufacturing process secrets.

We called ourselves the Citizens Against Chlorine Contamination, or CACC. Early on, we all contemplated the hardball nature of our opponent and the possibility of a SLAPP, or "strategic lawsuit against public participation," aimed at shutting us up and making us go away. Scott arranged for the CACC to be incorporated into the Utah chapter of the Sierra Club as a "working committee" so we were guaranteed a defense if we were sued.

From the beginning, the CACC was a natural team with a gift for dividing labor and spelling one another when relief was needed. Best of all, it was a group that was low on egos and high on humor. Meetings, even at times of crisis concerning grim issues, always included lots of wit and easy laughter. CACC members enjoyed each other and became friends. Ecoactivism can be hard and thankless work on high-stakes issues that is done during precious hours after work at the expense of family and recreation. Humor and friendship can mitigate those circumstances radically.

The CACC often resembled a dynamic and savvy tag-team. When Erin moved to Oregon, Kathy Van Dame, who could immediately and thoroughly research any question that came up, jumped in to replace her. Both the core group and the advisory group were kept in the loop via e-mail so that they could pitch in with research, advice, contacts, and encouragement when needed. It was a different experience than the struggle I had overcoming fear, sickness, and inexperience when trying to get Tooele County residents organized and moving.

Like most vigorous struggles against polluters, ours took place on several fronts. Each front opened with a key question. In mid-1996, for example, Magcorp was asking the state for permission to increase production. The documentation they submitted claimed there would be a very minimal corresponding increase in pollution. This begged the question "how do they figure they can do that?" The answer was simple. Magcorp's original I G Farben technology for splitting magnesium chloride electrolitically is old, outdated, and leaks like a sieve. Magcorp planned to increase production by adding new "sealed-cell" production units that cut way down on "fugitive emissions." This, in turn, begged another question: why isn't the state of Utah pressuring Magcorp to replace the old dirty technology with the new and cleaner sealed-cell technology? This also seemed to make sense from a business perspective as the new cells were far more efficient and allowed the company to cut the electricity it used, a major cost factor.

I approached state legislators and asked if they would be open to helping Magcorp to invest in new clean technology. Carrots, I reasoned, can be as important as sticks. Magcorp was already using public land under dirt-cheap deals and taking advantage of every tax break and loophole available to the mining industry, a case study in corporate welfare, but I looked anyway. I learned there were existing tax exemptions to encourage investment in new technology. I also found there were cheap loans available. Unfortunately, carrots are fairly useless if you cannot locate the mule you are trying to lead. Magcorp made clear that it was not going to sit down at the table and discuss such private matters as its investment in technology with mere citizens, who Magcorp President Lee Brown characterized in Salt Lake's major daily newspapers as "mean and ignorant" people who were "picking" on them. Several state officials expressed interest in getting talks going so Magcorp could be offered incentives for cleaning up, but they never succeeded in leading them to the table.

We also had another burning question. Why does a plant that has redundancy built into every aspect of production so that it never shuts down, even for a day, have only one pollution control device, especially since that device has a clear history of wearing out and breaking down? It had at least two of everything else it needed, so why not a back-up chlorine reduction burner? We eventually took this question to the Utah Air Quality Board.

The Utah Air Quality Board is a dubious example of stakeholder involvement. It is a group of representatives from the industries monitored and regulated by the Division of Air Quality who oversee the very agency that regulates them. The Air Quality Board also includes a citizen representative. Obviously, the advantage and benefit of the doubt in such an incestuous governance structure goes to industry. Even so, the AQ Board agreed with the CACC and the Utah Department of Environmental Quality's director, Dianne Nielson, who argued our case with us. Magcorp's representatives were furious and stormed out of the hearing. They made it plain that there was no way they'd agree to such an unreasonable and unwarranted demand. Too expensive! And, of course, the state shrugged and claimed there was no way it could force Magcorp to make it happen.

After the AQ Board made its toothless "request," I heard confidentially from an attorney for Utah industry who claimed that Utah's other industries wanted "something done" about Magcorp, even at the risk of setting precedents they might later regret. They had made big painful investments in new technology to comply and clean up. They were fearful and resentful that Magcorp's rotten apple example was giving them all an undeserved putrid aroma.

To the credit of the Utah Department of Environmental Quality, Magcorp did become a priority as we pushed them to make it so. Our relations were usually cordial and cooperative with the state. They went out of their way to keep us informed. In any government regulatory agency you can find employees who are frustrated by the bureaucratic inertia they face and chafed by the political constraints they work under. They know they should do more to translate their mission into action and they will do more if provided with political cover to do so. In Magcorp's case, there was an obvious bad guy, an unrepentant offender with a reputation so foul that even its allies held their noses in its presence.

Other questions concerned the rigged rules Magcorp seemed to operate under. For example, the so-called "Unavoidable Breakdown Rule" removed any incentive for Magcorp to build redundancy into its pollution abatement system because it gave them permission to operate outside the boundaries of its pollution allowances as long as the breakdown of its equipment was "unavoidable." Just about anything qualified as unavoidable. More questions involved the EPA's responsibility for regulating Magcorp. For example, what kind of standards would it set for chlorine emissions? Should EPA be allowed to look at that refinery in Norway that did a comparatively excellent job of controlling emissions when it set the MACT for magnesium refineries? Should magnesium refineries be placed on the EPA's "dioxin list" and monitored carefully for those emissions? Each inquiry notched up the pressure on Magcorp and its state and federal regulators to put teeth into the rules. The judicious use of attorneys to raise such questions guaranteed attention.

The most important question of all was: what about dioxins? Dioxins are produced when chlorine is burned. Obviously, a lot of chlorine was being burned. Magcorp so adamantly denied it produced dioxins that Cindy King of the Sierra Club lost her adjunct teaching job at Salt Lake Community College when she dared to suggest they did and Lee Brown leaned on the college's administration to clean up their faculty. As for the state agencies charged with protecting the environment and the public health that flowed from it, they had simply never bothered to look. Nobody asked them to. No squeak, no grease.

When Scott Endicott presented the state with a thorough analysis of the chemistry of Magcorp's production process that conclusively demonstrated how dioxin must be a byproduct, along with documentation from the Norway refinery showing dioxin creation, the state agreed that testing was appropriate. We then argued for almost two years on how to do that.

Scott, Howard, and Deep Throat insisted that a logical place to verify the creation of dioxins would be the "scrubber liquor" that would come out of Magcorp's pollution abatement system. We had heard that sludges, waste waters, packing, and filters from the pollution abatement system ("pollution control" would be an exaggeration) were packed into barrels and disposed of in a variety of ways. While hiking along the base of Stansbury Island, on the edge of the land Magcorp leased from the BLM, I had seen half-buried rusting barrels. It was not hard to imagine the lax ways those contaminated barrels could be distributed into a highly corrosive lakeside environment. Barrels that rusted open would leak their contents on to ground that dried up and blew around in the hot summer sun or was flushed by rising lake water in the spring.

The release of scrubber water from the pollution abatement system into ditches and holding ponds was another likely vector. Ground water could be contaminated. The most likely "vectors" for dioxin to get out into the world were not the smokestacks but from inside the plant, barrel by barrel or drop by drop.

Once again, we were confronted by a startling example of how a global economy and the food chain make us all downwind and downstream from one another. Dioxins are "hydrophobic." They don't stay in water if they can find a flesh ride out. If dioxins got into the lake's water, then, they could find their way out by getting into brine shrimp. The brine shrimp are commercially harvested and fed to prawns. The prawns are sold on an open market to those who desire them. Dioxins from Magcorp, then, could contaminate Great Salt Lake brine shrimp that are fed to prawns that are then fed to Japanese consumers who have never even heard of Magcorp or considered why they should care how it is operated.

When the state finally agreed with CACC that they should look for dioxins where they would logically find them, using methods that were scientifically well established, Magcorp finally admitted it probably produced dioxins, but insisted they would be no problem to others unless released from its stack. They knew that the Norwegian magnesium refinery had been thoroughly examined for dioxins and 99 percent of the dioxins found were on particulates in waste water emissions. Only 1 percent of the dioxins they produced left the plant in air emissions. So Magcorp insisted on stack testing. They also knew that looking for dioxins in smokestack emissions was difficult, especially when such volumes of chlorine gas were present. The chances of getting a misleading "false negative" reading were high. Magcorp was so anxious to play the testing card that was most likely to turn up in its favor that they even offered to pay for testing costs. This set off another round of debate and more delays. Ecoactivism is almost always a process of two steps forward, one step back.

In the summer of 1998, the tide began to turn. That spring we visited the editorial boards of the *Salt Lake Tribune* and the *Deseret News*. The core group met on a rainy morning in the lobby of the gleaming new *Deseret News* office tower in downtown Salt Lake. We had a hard time recognizing one another as we had each shed a scruffy LL Bean demeanor for coats, ties, shined shoes and, in Erin's case, a dress. I noticed we all retained a rumpled air despite our efforts, but we had done our best to show respect and look credible. We took an elevator to the top and were ushered into the oddly sumptuous new boardroom. We sat in huge upholstered chairs across a massive round table from the editorial board. As we prepared to talk, we realized that a clear image of the earth shone on the dark wood table surface in front of each chair, the reflection of an elaborate glass carving of the globe that was softly backlighted on the ceiling above us.

We made our case in the usual CACC style. Each person gave background and developed our case as suited his or her own passion or expertise. Questions were quickly referred to the person in the group with the most understanding in that area. I did overview and context quickly. Howard knew the permitting issues and the political intricacies of environmental policies and rules. Scott explained the chemistry of dioxin formation and the science of testing. Deep Throat pitched in on how the plant is put together and operates, careful not to disclose trade secrets. Erin emphasized the health impacts that were at stake.

Our bottom-line message was that we wanted to talk to Magcorp. That's how issues are resolved in America, we argued. People come together, state their needs and work towards creative win–win resolutions. Give us a chance to show Magcorp how reasonable we can be. We had crafted an appeal for dialogue and sent it to Magcorp but we were promptly rebuffed. At one point in our meeting, an editorial board member who had been thumbing through copies of the Magcorp correspondence that responded to our formal offer to meet, interrupted the discussion to tap at the letter before him and declare, "this is a remarkable piece of communication!" He then expressed his surprise at the gruff and negative tone of Magcorp's letter. It was not so much the idea that a corporation refused to talk to citizens downwind who swallow their emissions that riled him, but the notion that men occupying that level of corporate power would be so rude in their public correspondence. It wasn't even a violation of what he considered appropriate and civil corporate behavior that offended him. He was amazed by how unsavvy they were. Once again, Magcorp was helping us make our case by playing the role of West Desert Pirate. "What pollution?! Aargh!"

Two weeks later the *Deseret News* ran an editorial entitled "Time for Magcorp to Come to the Table." It was, of course, unheeded by the peglegged crew at Magcorp's corporate offices. That was expected. The strategic reason for wanting the editorial was simple. With the opinion of the *Deseret News* on our side and in print, we could go over the heads of those Magcorp officers who had rebuffed us and write directly to that guy Ira Rennert in Rockefeller Plaza. We would say, "hey, you've got a problem in Utah and your boys out there are blowing it." We wanted to start a fire behind Magcorp's line of defense. But our offer to talk was not a ploy. If the decisions we make about what we allow into our air, water, and soil get translated into flesh and blood downwind and downstream, then a decision-making process that is informed, inclusive, and open is better than one that is unaware, narrow, and closed. Pollution issues always boil down to who gets to sit at the decision-making table and how soon they get there. Magcorp needed to rethink how it operated and we wanted to be there when they did so.

I wrote the letter to Rennert. At the end of it, I made a veiled threat that the same bad reputation that Magcorp enjoyed would also be shared by Renco if talks did not ensue. It was an idle threat. I had talked to a reporter at *Time* magazine about the story and he had gone so far as hiring a photographer to fly over the plant and snap photos, but he left for another magazine and the story went with him. We weren't sure where to go next.

Then Michael Shnayerson called. Shnayerson was writing an article for the August '98 issue of *Vanity Fair* magazine about a zoning battle on Long Island. Some guy named Ira Rennert wanted to build an ocean-liner sized mansion in the middle of a quaint and quiet village of artists, fishermen, and potato farmers. If fishermen and farmers were all that Rennert had to contend with, his mansion would have been a quick done deal. But Sagaponack is part of the Hamptons, weekend home to millionaires. Such Hollywood powers as Steven Spielberg, Tommy Mottola, and Barry Sonnenfeld have homes nearby. So do Alec Baldwin and Kim Basinger. So do Ed and Caroline Kennedy Schlossberg and writers Peter Mathiesson and Kurt Vonnegut.

Until Rennert arrived on the scene, most of those who "discovered" the Hamptons appreciated its rural laid-back qualities. It was a place to escape the pace and noise of nearby New York City, or the pretensions and competition of places like Beverly Hills. Homes were supposed to be modest and compatible with the historic colonial village setting. Even when corporate and banking chiefs like Barry Trupin, Max Lerner, and Robert Hurst built mansions, they tended to be modest by the standards of America's power elite. Rennert's dream house, however, was designed to go into the record books.

Twice the size of the White House, more than twice the size of the famous high-tech house of Bill Gates near Seattle, the villa that Rennert planned was mall-like in scale. The main building would be 66,000 square feet. With "out buildings," the footage total went up to 100,000. That included more than forty bedrooms, twenty-nine bathrooms, three dining rooms, two libraries, two bowling alleys, squash, tennis, and basketball courts, a servants' wing, and a 200-car garage, all of it behind two imposing gatehouses and a sixteen-foot hedge.

Neighbors were appalled. Rennert's villa would take up sixty-three of the last acres of open field in the community of Sagaponack, dwarfing surrounding homes and dominating the ocean-front landscape. As they looked at the plans and asked themselves "who is this guy?," many concluded that Rennert was not building a house at all. Rennert, they learned, was a major donor to several orthodox Jewish causes and was also associated with controversial militant groups.

Oddly enough, while Rennert was consigning workers to forty hours a week in Hell and treating downwind citizens and wildlife as if they were expendable, he was giving out expensive Torahs and ingratiating himself to spiritual and human rights leaders like Elie Wiesel. He owned one of the most expensive homes in Jerusalem on the end of a crooked lane called Ethiopia Street, a short walk from the Old City. It was Rennert who, right after the election of Benjamin Netanyahu as Israeli premier, financed a controversial plan to open a long-closed tunnel near the Wailing Wall and Aqsa Mosque in Jerusalem. The riots that resulted disrupted the peace process and left seventy dead and hundreds wounded.

What if the Rennert villa was really a means of building a training or conference center for a militant orthodox Jewish group in the guise of a private dwelling? What if he was really building a compound for visiting Israeli heads of state like Netanyahu? The fact that many of his outraged neighbors were reform Jews added another layer of subtle contention to the controversy. Here was a man who supported groups that had questioned their rights and status as Jews in Israel.

The would-be neighbors organized. Surely, they and their lawyers argued, Sagaponack's zoning laws would be violated by such a pretentious monstrosity as Rennert's dream house. But Rennert's lawyers had done their homework. They took advantage of zoning laws that were designed to address those problems and controversies anticipated for modest mansions on one- to two-acre lots. For example, by making sure the blueprints described a house no more than thirty-two feet high, they avoided the need for variances. The residents of the Hamptons had designed their zoning codes to protect against riff raff and gauche starter-castles, but never considered the need to protect against would-be homeowners who were richer than they were and willing to break the unspoken rules of their club. Consequently, the local zoning codes had holes in them. Wherever there was a loophole, Rennert and his lawyers drove right through it. Approval was given and then challenged. In 1999, the original approval was confirmed but the battle continued.

As Shnayerson investigated how Rennert's mansion meteor had burned a hole through the zoning atmosphere above the Hamptons and left a large crater in the local sensibilities, he too asked, "who is this guy?" He began by examining how the man acquired the kind of wealth that permitted such royal extravagance. Financial analysts Shnayerson talked to agreed that if Ira took his private company public, he could increase his wealth tenfold. But then he'd have to put up with nosy shareholders and meddling reporters going through his financial records and asking awkward questions.

Rennert's unwillingness to give up a secretive and exclusive life behind the Ira Curtain, even in exchange for adding millions of dollars to his precious fortune, may be explained by the nature of his businesses. Rennert, Shnayerson discovered, made his fortune by finding industrial operations so environmentally repugnant that they are considered undesirable and burdensome investments by the other captains of our economy and are, therefore, under-priced bargains. His deals include a dirty steel mill in Ohio, the Doe Run lead mining operation in Missouri, and another mining operation in Peru. The steel mill was the site of a bitter strike in 1995 that included scabs and "goon guards." The lead mining operation in Missouri once threatened the watersheds for the last wild rivers in the Ozarks. The Peru operation is also commonly described as a scene from Hell. Rennert has since been dubbed the biggest private polluter in America. A man with such dubious acquisitions doesn't appreciate scrutiny or shareholder democracy.

After he collects his toxic trophies, Rennert simply pays fines levied by environmental regulators that are designed to encourage compliance with the law and public policy, or he fights them aggressively in court. To Renco, fines are just another cost of doing business and, apparently, a cost that is less than the expense of cleaning up its dirty act. Regulators are in good company. Rennert also turns his back on critics and reporters alike. When muckraking film producer Michael Moore, of *Roger and Me* fame, attempted to find and interview Rennert, he was slapped with a restraining order. He ignores neighbors, too, unless you count the *in abstentia* efforts of his lawyers. To those of us who have tried to open a dialogue with him, his silence speaks contempt. Shnayerson described the experience of researching Rennert's holdings as "rather like lifting a rock to see squirmy creatures underneath."

After he researched Ira's ill-gotten gain, Shnayerson looked for sources who could give his story a personal angle. That led him to us. I talked to Michael, sent him a packet of articles and documents, and gave him the phone numbers of others who could help him fit our piece of the Rennert puzzle. Then I called John Hollenhorst, a local television reporter I trusted, and used the *Vanity Fair* article as bait to encourage a story on local television. He was on a plane a few days later and an excellent three-part series followed.

We tried hard that summer to paint Ira's face all over Magcorp. It was hard for people to understand the mechanics behind the need for a redundant chlorine reduction burner, to understand the protocols of dioxin testing, or to understand the intricacies of the Unavoidable Breakdown Rule. But greed and selfishness are always easy to recognize. The Magcorp story suddenly hit the public consciousness as a simple tale about choice. A selfish man chose a massive mansion for himself over clean air for all of us. That was not an unfair way to frame the issue. It is actually how these choices are always made. Someone or some small group enjoys power and privilege that they do not want to give up in return for the common good. In the case of Magcorp, the characters in the story and the choices they faced were simply more clearly defined and revealed.

The state finally agreed to test Magcorp from the inside out, but they insisted they would start by nibbling on the edges. Soil and water samples were taken along a wastewater ditch that ran to a settling pond just outside the refinery. Other samples were taken outside the waste path to get a reading on background levels of dioxin. Magcorp stood by while the state tested. The CACC, of course, was not invited.

When the results came back, they were unambiguous. Dioxin showed up in the ditch at thirty-nine parts per billion. One part per billion is a dioxin level that the Centers for Disease Control consider high enough to trigger a full-blown clean up effort. When dioxins were found in Times Beach, Missouri, at similar levels found next to Magcorp, the town was evacuated. The results were alarming even to the state of Utah. More testing was planned immediately. The EPA agreed to chip in. Magcorp saw the writing on the wall and agreed to cooperate. Game over.

After the results were released, a reporter called for an "I told you so" statement. Vindication was satisfying but short-lived. A complete series of tests would still have to follow and experience told us that we'd have to watchdog the process so the state did not drop the ball. Key questions remained unanswered. If dioxin-contaminated waste was removed, where did it go? If it went to landfills, did the landfill operators know what they had on their hands and act accordingly? What would the state or EPA require Magcorp to do about its dioxin problem?

Another compelling question concerned worker safety. If dioxin-laden waste was packed into barrels, who packed it and were they exposed? The Utah's Department of Environmental Quality passed that one on to the workplace safety regulators, who, in their best Occupational Health and Safety Administration parody yet, have decided the workers are actually in a "safe haven" since they assume the dioxin goes out and away from the stack that the workers toil under. The only thing worse than having no government agency to step in and protect worker health and safety is pretending you have one when you don't. If Magcorp was using ladders that violated some standard they had set, OHSA would have been on them like white on rice. That's the kind of violation that a bureaucrat with a clipboard has the confidence to point out and write up. But a workplace contaminated with dangerous dioxins was a big and scary violation, the kind of challenge that called for willful ignorance and denial.

Never underestimate the power of the marketplace. The testing results were well covered by the media and mostly called alarming. Magcorp's competitors were gleefully spreading the bad news, too. In the wake of the news, the customers for Magcorp's chemical byproducts and recycled chemicals began challenging the company to certify that its products were dioxin free. Tough Magcorp officers who stood ready to confront regulators and ignore citizen activists wilted and then wailed when their bottom line was threatened. Suddenly Magcorp wanted testing fast. Maybe too fast. In the winter of 1999, they were getting ready to do a kind of unreliable stack testing that would resolve nothing. Still refusing to open the door to opponents and enter dialogue, Magcorp continued to build its strategy in the dark.

In the spring of 1999, Magcorp officers finally agreed to invite activists to their corporate headquarters for a chat with the state sitting in and ready to referee. Scott, Kathy, and I represented CACC. We met in the company's plain and modest headquarters building on the western edge of Salt Lake City. Everyone was on his and her best behavior. Magcorp's reps were casually attired in bluejeans, boots, and workshirts. They ushered us into a no-frills conference room which could have doubled as a break room. They talked and we listened politely.

Talking to citizens was a big step for them and we wanted it to be a positive experience.

They described a second round of dioxin testing they had conducted with some oversight from the state. The results showed very high readings again in waste ditches and piles around the refinery. They had also collected soil samples from gutters around Salt Lake's Pioneer Park that also revealed high dioxin contamination. They did not explicitly claim that the high levels of dioxin in these unsolicited urban samples excused their dioxin contribution, but told us they had collected the additional samples to "add to our perspective."

Yes, they conceded, the latest results confirmed a dioxin presence around the facility, but they hastened to argue that they were sure the waste piles were stable, there would be no dioxin migration, and over time the dioxin would break down in sunlight and fade away. In the meantime, no new dioxin would be added because they had figured out how to eliminate it from their production process. This, of course, involved precious proprietary information that they were reluctant to reveal.

They saved the best news for last. Plant manager Ron Thayer could barely contain a grin as he described new "multi-polar" processing technology that would cut energy costs by a third and result in magnesium so pure he described it as "honey." The new technology went well beyond the efficiency of the "sealed cell" electrolitic technology they had installed two years earlier when we began our effort to get them to clean up. Pollution could be cut by 90 percent in as little as two years. This was not something Magcorp wanted to commit to until final results on the new technology were in, probably by the fall of 1999, but they were very optimistic and would definitely make a multimillion-dollar investment if the news was good.

It was clear to us that gaining a competitive advantage was something Magcorp understood and would invest in. A dramatic cut in pollution was a side benefit, one that they hoped would please us and make us go away. When change comes, of course, they will say "we were always going to do it" and the role of citizen action in pushing them to go farther sooner will not be acknowledged. That's the way it works. The CACC was hopeful and optimistic but still saying "seeing is believing." We heard from other activists who had dealt with Ira Rennert that he ignores critics until he can't avoid them, then makes promises until they relax their guard, and then continues his bad act as usual. All the talk of technology could be a ploy. Much remained to be done, but the eventual outcome is certain. Magcorp will clean up.

Much has been said recently about taking a second look at how we charter corporations and the rights they enjoy at the expense of citizens. Such discussions can lead to useful strategies to create new laws and policies that ensure corporate accountability and redefine the relationship between citizen, community, and corporation. But each situation on the ground is different and requires its own strategy, its own mix. Every corporation exists in a community with a particular set of complex conditions and relationships. Public attitudes vary according to how the company employs us, pays its taxes, pollutes, and contributes to our charities, and whether it makes a product we want and need. Some corporations are more successful at purchasing access to decision makers than others. Some have the resources and know-how to influence us and some, like Magcorp, don't have a clue. It takes local citizens to understand the corporation's standing in its community, to sort it all out and find the handles that will curb private polluters. In every incident where a big private polluter was made accountable, there is one common variable—local citizen activists. Laws alone do not work.

In the defense of public health and environmental integrity, local citizen activists are the catalysts and the bottom line. We are like a keystone species in the political ecosystem and we are always endangered. But our numbers and power are bound to grow. My children's generation grew up with the ecological lessons baby boomers had to learn on their own the hard way. We baby boomers will be retiring soon and we'll have lots of time for political adventure. Our children will join us. Magcorp is already a relic.

TEN

BETTING THE RANCH
AT THE NUCLEAR CASINO

As usual, the fat cats' government has a plan. Critics call it "Mobile Chernobyl." If they can't force it through, Private Fuel Storage has an alternate plan. Nuclear Plan B could land 2,000 canisters of spent nuclear fuel in Margene Bullcreek's backyard. Literally. In a few years, if the consortium of Midwest and other powerful utilities represented by PFS gets its way, Margene could step outside her home and pitch a rock at big fat containers of nuke waste. That wouldn't be wise, of course, since spent fuel rods from nuclear reactors will be lethally hot for at least 10,000 years and radioactive for about 250,000 years, at least ten times as long as America's aboriginal people, the Goshutes, have been living on their ancestral desert ground.

Margene stands in the doorway of her modest frame house, one among a small isolated cluster of homes in the middle of the 18,000-acre Skull Valley Reservation. She shades her eyes from the sun and looks out at the sagebrush ocean that laps at her steps. "Cedar and Sage are sacred here. I cut willow branches over there to cradle my babies like my mother did, and my grandmother did, and her mother and her mother. Their bones are on this land. If you think this is desolate then you don't know the land. You don't know how to be still and listen. There is peace here."

Leon Bear lives across the rutted gravel road. Recently, he has taken to wearing expensive blue suits and talking on cell phones from his new car. These are habits he and his Tribal Council associates picked up while touring Europe to learn about the nuclear power industry and how safe it is. They were guests of PFS and wined and dined by the nuclear power elite who created PFS when federal plans to obtain a temporary storage site failed. Leon is the Tribal Council chairman. Margene leads Ohngo Gaudadeh Devia, the community-based organization that opposes PFS and Leon Bear to protect "Sogobia," or Mother Earth. They are not neighborly anymore.

If "traditional" Goshutes like Margene still honor their roots in the American aboriginal dreamtime, Leon's dreams look more like those of any white stockbroker or banker. He is tired of poverty and the absence of opportunity. He thinks big. In 1987, it was a $6 billion "supercollider" made of giant underground magnets to explore the substructure of atoms. That fell through and was replaced by a proposal to site a massive "gravitational wave observatory." When that vision faded from his decoder ring, he and his clan allies settled for a simple recycling plant in Bauer, just south of Tooele. That project went bankrupt. Leon may be the only businessman on the planet who failed at recycling glass bottles and aluminum cans who has been given a second chance, this time to juggle nuclear fuel rods.

After the recycling plant went belly-up, noise was made about a gambling casino, a scheme that had certainly worked on other reservations. Just over the Nevada–Utah border in

Wendover, only fifty miles from Skull Valley, casinos do a thriving business with Utah customers who are forbidden to place bets in their own state or even buy wine at a grocery store. Popular Nevada bumper stickers say, "Eat, drink, and be merry—for tomorrow you will be in Utah." Unfortunately for Leon Bear and company, Utah's patriarchal Legislature, the vigilant guardians of a strict religious code, will not tolerate gambling in their state, unless it is the kind done with chemical weapons incinerators and downwind prawn farmers.

Skull Valley is wide and dry, about fifty miles west of Salt Lake, where the transition between the forested ecosystems of the big mountains fade into the high desert ecosystem of the Great Basin. Go one valley to the east and you might claim you are not on a desert. When you get to Skull Valley, there is no doubt. It is not attractive for farming or even grazing, though cows do wander through the parched brush. One of the first settlements in the valley was Iosepa, a colony for early Hawaiian converts to Mormonism who were set apart. Some were lepers whose diseases were not apparent until after they reached Zion. Iosepa means Joseph, after the Mormon prophet Joseph Smith. Then the Goshutes rebelled against settler encroachment in the 1860s and were sent there to give up their hunting and gathering ways and learn to farm. In 1968, after a nerve agent test at nearby Dugway Proving Grounds went awry and killed 6,400 sheep, the carcasses were buried somewhere on Goshute land, though no one can recall exactly where. In the last decade, a notorious family of polygamists have settled just up the road from the reservation, far from the authorities who bug them. Skull Valley has a long history of hiding something.

No wonder then that PFS should find Leon Bear and Skull Valley. The reservation's council had raised its hand and volunteered earlier when the federal government was looking for a temporary storage site for all the backed-up used fuel rods crowding around the nation's one hundred plus nuclear reactors.

Fuel rods are long metal tubes packed with the ceramic-like pellets of enriched uranium and bundled together in groups of 200. During fission, a uranium isotope, U-235, is split apart and releases enough energy to boil water and make steam that turns a generator to make electricity. After a few years, when the fissionable material has been used up, the rods are "spent." They then go to a cooling pond which is actually a steel-lined concrete basin. After that, it gets problematic. The fuel rods are still very dangerous and will remain so for thousands of years. Who wants them for a neighbor? Who wants that liability? Nobody but Leon, apparently. While the cooling pools grew crowded and power companies resorted to moving the rods out of their watery baths and into "dry cask" storage on site, an ultimate solution could not be found. Storage costs were passed on to unhappy customers. Reactors started running out of room and the state and local governments around them turned up the pressure to ship the bad stuff away.

As is so often the case, the federal government stepped in to help public utilities dependent on nuclear reactors out of the poisonous corner they had painted themselves into. In 1986 the feds examined a possible site within a basalt and granite formation under the White Earth Reservation in Minnesota. The Minnesota Legislature responded by passing a law to block the disposal facility. The next year, the nuclear predators found easier pickings in Nevada at Yucca Mountain, a hundred miles northwest of Las Vegas and not far from the infamous test site for nuclear weapons. Yucca Mountain is in the backyard of the Western Shoshones who have been engaged in a protracted legal struggle over whether they surrendered their ancestral lands to the feds who have used them for nuclear testing. The Department of Energy discovered the advantage of driving through the breach the US military had already opened in the Shoshone wall. Never underestimate the power of precedence.

With the question of where to build the "permanent" repository behind them, Congress next created a national nuclear waste negotiator to set in motion a nationwide search for a temporary storage site to hold the spent fuel rods until Yucca Mountain could come online in 2010. It was authorized to contact communities at potential monitored retrievable storage, or MRS, sites and offer a lot of money. True to the well-established pattern, most of the targeted communities were Native American. About twenty took money to look the deal over, but only the Mescalero Apaches in New Mexico, the Fort McDermitt Reservation in Nevada, and the Skull Valley Goshutes got serious. The Nuclear Waste Policy Act forbids a temporary storage site and the permanent repository to be in the same state, so the McDermitt option was out. The Mescalero Apaches began feuding bitterly over whether to take the next step and Congress cut the program's funding.

Eventually, the government agencies looking for a temporary site, or MRS, decided that a location in Nevada near the Yucca Mountain permanent site would be best, despite the fact that national policy forbade it. The law would have to be changed. A political fight ensued. National opponents of the nuclear industry understood that the waste problem was intractable and a storage site, temporary or permanent, provided a relief valve that would allow the waste problem to build up again until the next impasse was reached. There is only so much desert. How much spent fuel can be swept under the Yucca rug before you run out of room and we start all over again? Opposition was even growing in normally complacent Nevada where most communities have no zoning and any government regulation is despised.

The utilities that held the waste watched in dismay. Spent fuel was piling up around their reactors and local citizens were getting nervous. Costs kept escalating. They decided they would have to take matters into their own hands. Consortiums formed to pool resources. Private Fuel Storage was the consortium formed by the Indiana-Michigan Power Company, Boston Edison, Consolidated Edison of New York, the Dairyland Power Cooperative, GPU Nuclear Corporation, Illinois Power, Northern States Power, Pacific Gas and Electric, Southern California Edison, Southern Nuclear Operating Company, and Wisconsin Electric Power. They took up where the feds left off and Leon Bear was waiting. The amount of money, $200 million by some estimates, that PFS had to hand out to a willing participant would go a long way among a small band like the Skull Valley Goshutes with only 149 members. Every member of the band might take a million-dollar cut.

In the meantime, things were not going well over at Yucca Mountain. The main contractor, TRW, was accused of sloppy work. At one point, the huge tunnel-boring machine, the Yucca Mucker, almost cut through the Ghost Dance Fault Zone which would have made the safety of the site unacceptable. Worse, serious and fundamental questions were raised about the wisdom of placing fuel rods that would be radioactive for more than 10,000 years within a geologic formation loaded with porous volcanic tuff, instead of the salt domes and hard rock formations originally recommended by the National Academy of Sciences. The $6.3 billion spent on exploration turned up evidence that the Yucca Mountain area is a Class Four earthquake zone, the second most active kind. Thirty-five faults run under the mountain and there have been about 600 small earthquakes recorded in the last twenty years. In June of 1992, a quake measuring 5.6 on the Richter Scale rocked Little Skull Mountain twelve miles away and did $250,000 of damage to a project building. No one is sure how all the fissures link together and what impact the constant pounding shocks from nuclear testing have had on geologic integrity over the years.

Volcanic eruptions are also a potential problem. Cinder cones along the surface of the site zone are evidence of the last volcanic eruptions that may have happened as recently as 2,000 years ago. If Yucca Mountain is as seismically active as suspected, then the next volcanic eruption could be man-made with radioactive fallout mixed with the ash that drifts downwind. Seismic or volcanic activity could easily change the course of underground water flow. The rods will be stored about 1,000 feet above and below major aquifers. Geologically, 1,000 feet is eggshell thin. Safe storage for 10,000 years not only assumes that 10,000 years is good enough, it assumes formations stay where they are, climate doesn't change, and the desert doesn't flood if it does.

Scientists recently got a remarkable demonstration of how

fluid our environment can be. More than a dozen new radio-active hot spots showed up on the 560 square mile Hanford, Washington, site where weapons-grade plutonium was manu-factured during the Cold War. Hanford, surrounded by Umatilla tribal land, is a nuclear nightmare, but the scientists thought they had mapped the hot spots and the new ones were baffling. They then realized they were looking at a case of "ecological transport." Contaminated worms and bugs, includ-ing fruit flies, ants, roaches, and gnats, were making the new hot spots as they moved about and lived their little lives.

Also near Hanford, the leaves of mulberry trees along the banks of the Columbia River, home of major salmon, steelhead, and sturgeon fisheries, were found to have about 4,000 times the amount of Strontium 90 that is considered safe for drinking water. No one is sure why. Radioactive water flowing from under the Nevada Test Site is also showing up where it wasn't supposed to be faster than it was supposed to travel.

Despite steady stream of bad news about the prospects for "permanent" storage generally, and the Yucca Mountain site specifically, the project continues. Utilities are powerful and they want a site, any site, now. The usual nuclear titans are now at the Yucca Mountain trough. Contractors include TRW, SAIC, Bechtel, Westinghouse, Sandia, and the Livermore and Los Alamos laboratories. History repeats itself. The Western Shoshone are outgunned again.

The lethal longevity of radioactive waste throws questions and expectations about risk into a time frame that is far broader than the usual civic or corporate plan, revealing the limited nature of our predictions and balance sheets. For example, where do you think the Stock Market will be in 10,000 years when the Yucca Mountain hiding place reaches the end of its dubious planned lifespan? What will be the cost then, in twenty-first-century dollars, to clean up contaminated aquifers? Dealing with such a virulent curse as nuke waste is forcing us to think in geologic, or Gaian, time. It puts us in Margene's backyard again, looking out on the old ways that teach respect and humility before an awesomely intricate natural world where animals, plants, and even rocks speak. We will not measure our way out of this crisis, especially if measurement is biased by self-interested power. We need science, but common sense, too.

Native American creation stories and myths may sound absurd to us who move and migrate, move and migrate, like our grandparents and their grandparents did. I have to go to a special research library to solve my genealogical mysteries and I will not discover I am rooted in a bear or spider. But native wisdom remembers the biological roots and the long human story we forgot and are only lately rediscovering with our satellites and labs. Grace Thorpe, daughter of the great athlete Jim Thorpe and leader of a campaign to get Native Americans to declare their lands "Nuke Free Zones," tells a cautionary tale passed down from Navajo ancestors about their origins. When passing from the last world to this one, the people were given a choice. They could take the yellow dust from the rocks or the yellow dust of corn pollen. The people chose corn pollen and were nourished. The Gods warned them to leave the other yellow dust in the ground or it would bring evil. For hundreds of thousands of years, human beings survived their evolutionary journey by relying on accumulated wisdom and well-honed intuition. But when a common uncredentialed Indian like

Margene Bullcreek stands before the scientific and technical elite and says, "we need to protect our Mother Earth because we are empty without her," she is politely tolerated and then condescendingly dismissed out of hand.

Thank goodness for white allies. Utah governor Mike Leavitt, well known in environmental circles for his pathetic wilderness proposals and his attempt to pave Great Salt Lake wetlands with the Legacy Highway, grew up in Cedar City. He rose from modest rural roots to earn a fortune in the insurance business and become a top lobbyist and broker in Utah politics, like his dad, Dixie. He is a clean cut and tidy man, the kind we like in Utah. His public presentations are careful, articulate, and reserved. But in the winter of 1998, I sat next to him at a witness table before a subcommittee of the Utah State Legislature and saw him drop his guard. He was telling legislators why he wanted to seize the Tooele County road that runs from I-80 through Skull Valley. He knew, although he did not say it, that Tooele County commissioners were sniffing around the same deal Leon Bear accepted from PFS and that PFS would eventually find their price. If the state took the road, Leavitt would make sure trucks hauling nuclear waste would not roll down it. Leavitt had finished his prepared speech and, prompted by a question, talked about the Southern Utah relatives he had lost to cancer. A hint of "over-my-dead-body" passion rose to his surface. Leavitt, it became clear, is a downwinder.

The legislators were moved, and one by one also bore their testimony. Some had lost parents, others siblings. Everyone had lost someone. They voted to give the state the road. That spring,

Margene and I stood on either side of the governor as he pulled the cover off a sign at the head of the Skull Valley Road forbidding trucks carrying nuclear materials to pass. It was a photo op, of course, but it also recorded the hard passage of one man's life from innocent victim to wary defender.

The Tooele commissioners got mad and then they got busy. Commissioner Teryl Hunsaker, with typical bellicose bluster, threatened to build another road on county land parallel to the one the guv seized. Rail routes in were also explored. When Leon, PFS, and the commissioners thought they had found a back-door corridor across the Cedar Mountains to the west, Leavitt enlisted the help of his previous arch-enemies, the Southern Utah Wilderness Alliance, to identify tracts of wilderness that would be violated. The struggle over access to the Skull Valley Goshute land was becoming a festival of strange bedfellows and reversed roles. When the Nuclear Regulatory Commission came to town to hear input on the planning process for studying the site, no fewer than a dozen state regulators, including several division directors, trooped up to the hearing microphone and had the kind of knee-knocking public speaking experience that citizen activists endure when they testify before those same regulators. For activists like myself who invest much energy getting those regulators to be assertive, it was disorienting to step aside as they walked up to the mike and then cheer them on.

As the spring of 1999 blossomed across the Skull Valley floor, the moves and countermoves continued. Nuke chess in the desert promised to go on forever. Maybe that was the point. Leavitt hoped to wear down his PFS opponents, overwhelm them with new barriers, and stall their plans until the Yucca

Mountain disputes were resolved or another solution showed up. PFS had to keep probing the state's defenses until they found a way through or another less determined administration came along.

Environmental racism is a concept that was developed to describe the placement of toxic wastes and industries in minority communities. In the nuclear hall of mirrors constructed across the Great Basin, however, anything can appear as its opposite. Leon Bear decries the "racism" of those who oppose letting him accept nuclear waste. He says they violate his band's sovereignty. Margene pierces the reflections and sets the image right. "Sovereignty isn't selling your independence and your heritage to the highest bidder. What choice will we have after they park all that radioactive waste on our land?"

Leon has a point, too. The economic plight of the Goshutes was long ignored. If the state had paid half as much attention to the tribe's poverty as they do now to their plans to get rich quick, they wouldn't be in the mess they are now in. Goshutes have as much right to get rich as Khosrow Semnani.

Semnani is the owner of Envirocare, a low-level radioactive waste dump within the neighboring West Desert Hazardous Industries Area. Envirocare is becoming the national magnet for low-level nuclear waste, like medical and lab debris, contaminated soils, and uranium tailings. The growing effort to clean up military production complexes, mining and milling sites, and laboratory facilities is facing the same disposal bottlenecks experienced for spent fuel from commercial reactors. There is too much waste and too few places to put it. That is, there are very few places to bury it that have not been blocked by those local citizens and their governments who are unwilling to trade the risks of taking it for the business it brings.

Semnani had the good business sense to locate his dump in the right place at the right time. In the late eighties, the pattern for the West Desert was set, the locals were eager to deal, critics were few and far between, and the market was big and open. Still, Semnani ran into bureaucratic barriers. The burgeoning nuclear waste industry was beset by rules, tests, and complicated legal hurdles. Success required an expanded and enhanced permit from the state. Semnani gave $600,000 in cash, coins, and condos to Larry Anderson, Utah's chief nuclear regulator. Anderson claims the money and gifts were legitimate payments for consulting services he provided to help Envirocare get through a permitting maze. Anderson even sued Semnani when he failed to follow through with the final payments Anderson expected. Semnani admits he paid Anderson but claims he is the victim of extortion and, so far, the courts have backed his case.

Out-of-state nuke waste business competitors, and even wannabe competitors, jumped all over the Envirocare scandal in an attempt to cut some of Envirocare's business loose for themselves. Critics of the nuclear waste disposal business wonder aloud if the scandal is an isolated event, or if the habit of bribery creates an expectation that could be perceived as extortion. Courts will have to sort it all out while an embarrassed state government has cracked down on regulators and promised it won't happen again. Envirocare continues to thrive with the state's blessing.

Given the state's willingness to play ball with Envirocare despite such scandalous corruption, and their willingness to burn hazardous waste and chemical weapons, cooperate with biological war labs, and put up with nuclear testing all those years, the charge of hypocrisy is easy to make. In many ways, Leon Bear and company are only guilty of being the last ones through the door with the straw that broke the camel's back.

Margene was outnumbered from the beginning, at least among the Skull Valley band of Goshutes. The Goshute national government and those of surrounding tribes, like the Western Shoshone, have roundly condemned the PFS deal and support her. But there is a good reason Leon Bear and his associates control the Tribal Council in Skull Valley. They got elected. Only a handful of the band's members still live in Skull Valley. Most are in Wendover, Tooele, and Salt Lake City. They are trying in various ways and with varying success to assimilate, accommodate, understand, and cope with an acquisitive culture that utterly dominates them. They may feel badly about the bargain, but money dissolves resolve, especially if you know poverty. Becoming a millionaire, like the rich white characters you see on TV, by selling your claim to what you have already rejected to a white man, must seem like a delicious irony to Skull Valley Goshutes who moved into town long ago. Burn that bridge for a million bucks? Sure, where are the matches? For many of them, the PFS deal could be the last act of a slow cultural suicide. A traffic in souls, apparently, is part of the nuclear bargain.

Sometimes dreams become expectations and are keenly anticipated. Many Goshutes loyal to Leon Bear consider Margene Bullcreek a threat and an enemy. It is hard just to agree to disagree when the stakes are so high. Tensions on the

Skull Valley Reservation run high and the divisions grow deeper. Violence is possible where such bitterness abounds. The little Skull Valley cluster of homes ring with loud arguments. There have been assault charges filed. Doors are bolted at night. If PFS dropped its offer tomorrow, the Goshute community that banded together for thousands of years to face down drought, famine, and raiding warriors would be left as sclerotic with fissures as the ground beneath Yucca Mountain.

If the West Desert door is pried open to more nuclear waste, there will be no shortage of commerce. In addition to the 42,000 tons of spent commercial fuel already piled up around the nation's reactors, 2,000 tons more is produced each year. As it stands now, the commercial nuclear reactors will only stop producing the waste when they are decommissioned and their contaminated building materials are added to the bulk of radioactive debris from nuclear weapons processing sites. Then there is the 112 metric tons of plutonium from the 55,000 nuclear weapons we once aimed at the Soviet Union and its 70,000 weapons. Plutonium is both the Godzilla and Methuselah of the nuke monsters. One millionth of a gram can kill and it lives for 500,000 years.

For the people in Grantsville, Tooele, and Salt Lake City, the debate about waste policy may seem far removed from their daily lives. Skull Valley is almost fifty miles from Salt Lake City and hardly anyone ever goes there. Envirocare is even farther away. But they have not imagined the frequency or proximity of trucks and trains that will roll by their workplaces and homes carrying hot cargo. Fifty million people live within a half-mile of proposed truck and train routes to Yucca Mountain. If you live in St Louis, for example, one shipment will go through on average every eight hours for thirty years. According to Mary Olson of the Nuclear Information Resource Service, the passengers of a car traveling next to a truck loaded with nuke trash will receive the equivalent of one chest X-ray an hour. That kind of exposure presents a particularly dangerous risk for pregnant women, children, the elderly, and those with compromised immune systems. Accidents will happen, perhaps hundreds over the course of the Nuclear Waste Policy Act plan to bury it all under Yucca Mountain. Critics call the plan Mobile Chernobyl. Your tax dollars, by the hundreds of billions, will make it happen.

It is necessary to stop the madness, but just as important to question the uncritical assumptions that allowed it to stalk our lives. We have an odd way of calculating economic health in America. We believe the gross national product must always increase, even though it includes the good with the bad and even measures tragedy and madness as good for the economy. For example, say a school bus filled with little girls veers off a cliff and crashes. All are killed, a terrible tragedy. But someone will have to order a new school bus to be built and that makes jobs and revenue. Several little coffins will also be ordered. Then there are funeral services, flowers, and lots of litigation. All those lawyers will buy cars and vacation homes. Absurd? No more crazy than treating the nuclear industry, from weapons production to commercial reactors to waste disposal, as a measurable, predictable, and rational economic activity. Handling contamination and waste will create jobs, profits, and revenues. Decommissioning nuclear power plants and disposing of nuclear warheads will mean big business. But along the rim of America's Great Basin, we may be experiencing the last big economic boom before an endless toxic bust. A slow nuclear holocaust is unfolding across the globe as radiation from contaminated Cold War facilities like Hanford, Rocky Flats, and Mayakek in the former Soviet Union migrates outward and spent fuel rods escape their confines. If this is business as usual, we need to redefine "business" or redefine "usual."

In the beginning, according to the gospel of Nuclear Apocalypse, there was uranium. Most of it was found on indigenous people's treaty grounds. Native Americans were often persuaded to dig it out and the resulting exposure sickened them. They died in droves. The suffering and dying Indian miners were mostly ignored by the white power structure that could have helped them. The contamination of their food and drinking water from mine tailings was also unheeded. Above ground and then underground nuclear weapons testing was conducted on Western Shoshone doorsteps, exposing them to more risk than any other Americans. In return for their sacrifices, now that the nuclear wheel has turned far enough to produce lots of lethal waste and debris, Native Americans will be burdened with the worst poisons left at the end of the cycle. The evil yellow dust is returning.

Sadly the integrity of land assignments made to Native Americans after they were killed, starved, and sickened into submission was temporary. Those remote "wastelands" they were banished to at the end of the nineteenth century are now, at the end of the twentieth century, valuable for the very isolation that made them worthless a hundred years ago. Wherever their leaders can be plied with riches and sovereignty is for sale,

Native Americans are vulnerable to our shifting whims and needs and the next deal that comes with them. The bottom line is still a dead Indian. Genocide, apparently, is a hard habit to break. This time around, we may inadvertently kill our great-grandchildren, too.

If we don't snap out of it, our foolish and forgetful behavior will be tragic. We are fluid creatures whose eco-awareness has been obliterated by trauma, fear, and our all-consuming addictions to bigger, faster, and more. We are evolving into truly homeless beings, wandering through the dark and desperate for the next techno-fix. The signs of our failure and disconnection are littered across the desert floor. We are the newcomers here with our big thirsty cows, our broad highways and fast cars, our glittering casinos and horrific doomsday weapons, our booming jets and electronic battlefields, our war labs and bottomless toxic waste. When we gaze through the shimmering heat at the desert's vastness and proclaim it is an "empty wasteland," we are condemning it for craven use.

Perhaps our descriptions of deserts reveal more about ourselves than them. Margene is right. We make too much noise and we do not listen. She knows the desert is alive and beautiful. It is not desolate at all. Desolation is what we have carried to it.

AFTERWORD

In the past few years, many teenagers bearing video cassettes have trooped through my living room. Their taste in movie themes mirrors their life situation, precariously perched between the security of home and childhood and the challenges and uncertainties of adulthood. They cannot articulate their anxieties as they move out into the world, but they are revealed through the lights that flicker across my living-room walls. These kids know they inherit a perilous world beset by unprecedented crisis. In the movies they watch, the fears that are vague take on specific form and content—earthquakes, volcanoes, comets, alien invasions, satanic demons, dinosaurs misplaced in our era and run amok, slashers and serial killers who wear their victim's skin. Even Godzilla, that post-Hiroshima monster of atomic proportions, has come back.

This is the next generation raised in fear. Just as my generation had the Cold War sword of nuclear annihilation hanging by a thread over our heads, they live with the threat of ecotastrophe—global warming, the hole in the ozone layer, virus plagues—hanging over their lives. We had the Cuban missile crisis, the Berlin Wall, and the Vietnam War to remind us that our futures were threatened. They have had the Exxon Valdez, Chernobyl, and Aids casting shadows across their futures.

In the deserts of the American West, you can find clear signs that key aspects of our culture are not viable and may even be suicidal. If practicing nuclear, chemical, and biological warfare has left the land littered and contaminated with radiation and spores still dangerous after forty years, then war, as designed during the Cold War, is unwinnable and uncontainable. We seem to be learning that we cannot wage war against ourselves and the next generations. Chemical and biological weapons have now been outlawed by international treaty, though that monster is still not caged as long as a volatile world generates desperate terrorists. The poisonous remnants of Cold War weaponry will, of course, also haunt generations to come.

Likewise, our economy as currently designed also generates toxic and nuclear waste that is persistent and cannot be abided by human communities, wildlife, or watersheds. If we burned and dumped it in the desert to buy time for industrial solutions and alternatives to form and take hold, our collective behavior would at least have a rationale. But if we burn and bury to avoid the implications of our behavior altogether, then the consequences will eventually be on your doorstep as well as mine. Killer Waste, coming soon to a backyard near you. If you don't want to buy a ticket to that show, heed the canaries on the rim.

Perhaps it is healthy to vent your fears and the process may as well be entertaining, but we should also remind ourselves that we are not threatened by extraterrestrial insects, comets, or Jason rising from the grave with his claws. The real threats, the ongoing ones we try to deny because they are so hard to face, result from daily human activity that is considered normal, appropriate, and necessary. Aggregated, the enormity of that striving, getting, and using activity is overwhelming the planet's built-in ability to balance and heal. During my teenage days, we had a saying that originated in a popular cartoon strip of that era, "we have met the enemy and he is us." But the enemy is not us. It is not even man-made. It is "mind-made." It is one culture that is not inevitable or necessary. It is a culture that hides its waste and plays out its toxic fears in my backyard, poisoning as it goes. It is one culture that has worn out its welcome by going to extremes, but has also shown remarkable resiliency in the past and can shift again.

There are so many hopeful signs that we can recover our senses and find the courage we need to storm the pockets and towers of power and make meaningful change happen. Every day I look up and see another addicted and traumatized amnesiac relinquish his or her separateness from the world and find a way home. Remember we are human beings. We can always change our minds.

ACKNOWLEDGEMENTS

This book was written at home about activities that often took me away from home. For seven years, my family has tolerated and compensated for my absence and then they endured my obsession to capture my experiences in words. I am grateful for their approval and encouragement. Their love sustains me always. This is our book.

I also owe this book to Mike Davis. I met Mike a few years ago when he visited my home to learn about the legacy of military fallout and our struggle in a remote corner of Utah. His recognition of our accomplishments in the face of powerful odds was validating. We kept in touch. When he heard I had a manuscript, he jumped on it, then acted as both agent and editor. That first manuscript was substantially rewritten under Mike's wise guidance. I am thankful for his commitment, his generosity, and the intuitive rapport we enjoyed. I am in awe of Mike Davis and honored to receive his counsel.

The staff at Verso was helpful and easy. I am especially grateful to Colin Robinson and Amy Scholder for their patience and sound advice. I am proud to be associated with a publisher that puts purpose before profits and still succeeds.

Ecoactivism is a collective endeavor I have shared with too many to name. Closest to home, however, I must thank Sandy Covello and Janet Cook who have supported me throughout my strange quest and even took turns being the "village idiot" with me. Steve Erickson was an early and trusted mentor. Cindy King's dogged and consistent effort has made her a most reliable ally. Craig Williams is my most trusted advisor and constantly reminds me that activism requires humor as well as passion. I am in awe of Howard Gross and Scott Endicott for their policy expertise, scientific knowledge, and well-honed strategic senses. Erin Moore was both a steady comrade and early reader. Others who make a difference are Elizabeth Crowe, Melissa Tuckey, John Capillo, Lois Kleffman, Mick Harrison, Richard Condit, John Veranth, Kathy Van Dame, Lisa Puchner, Kenneth and Kim Smith, Jill Sheinberg, Jason Groenewold, Naomi Silverstone, John DeJong, Mark Graham, Ivan Weber, Nina Dougherty, Joro Walker, Lynn deFreitas, Rosemary Holt, Diane Olson Rutter, and Carrie Norton.

Steve Allen taught me about land use issues. He also restores my health and sanity each spring by leading me into the beautiful vast heart of Utah's wild canyonlands. There's no one I trust more on the other end of a rope when I am going over the edge.

Organizational support has also sustained me. Above all, the Sierra Club has consistently sheltered and steadfastly supported my political activities. Peter Montague and the Environmental Research Foundation are a constant source of information and enlightenment on toxic pollution and its impact on health. The members of Chemical Weapons Working Group,

Friends of the Great Salt Lake, the Military Toxics Project, the Southern Utah Wilderness Alliance, and the Center for Health, Environment and Justice are brothers and sisters in arms. Robert Redford and Patagonia provided early and key funding.

Finally, Bill and Lil's friendship and encouragement helped me move along and navigate the inevitable bumps in this road as well as all the others I have traveled in my life. The Hauze clan has not always understood my journey but they have always believed in my ability to describe it. Chris and Kevin, someday our songs will be published.

THE HAYMARKET SERIES

WAR AND TELEVISION *by Bruce Cumings*

IT'S NOT ABOUT A SALARY: Rap, Race and Resistance in Los Angeles *by Brian Cross, with additional texts by Reagan Kelly and T-Love*

CITY OF QUARTZ: Excavating the Future of Los Angeles *by Mike Davis*

PRISONERS OF THE AMERICAN DREAM: Politics and Economy in the History of the US Working Class *by Mike Davis*

THE ASSASSINATION OF NEW YORK *by Robert Fitch*

THE CULTURAL FRONT: The Laboring of American Culture in the Twentieth Century *by Michael Denning*

MECHANIC ACCENTS: Dime Novels and Working-Class Culture in America *by Michael Denning*

NOTES FROM UNDERGROUND: The Politics of Zine Culture *by Stephen Duncombe*

NO CRYSTAL STAIR: African Americans in the City of Angels *by Lynell George*

WHERE THE BOYS ARE: Cuba, Cold-War America and the Making of a New Left *by Van Gosse*

THE WAY THE WIND BLEW: A History of the Weather Underground *by Ron Jacobs*

POWER MISSES: Essays Across (Un)Popular Culture *by David E. James*

RACE, POLITICS AND ECONOMIC DEVELOPMENT: Community Perspectives *edited by James Jennings*

RACE AND POLITICS IN THE UNITED STATES: New Challenges and Responses for Black Activism *edited by James Jennings*

POSTMODERNISM AND ITS DISCONTENTS: Theories, Practices *edited by E. Ann Kaplan*

WHITE SAVAGES IN THE SOUTH SEAS *by Mel Kernahan*

SEVEN MINUTES: The Life and Death of the American Animated Cartoon *by Norman M. Klein*

THE HISTORY OF FORGETTING: Los Angeles and the Erasure of Memory *by Norman M. Klein*

RANK-AND-FILE REBELLION: Teamsters for a Democratic Union *by Dan La Botz*

MADE POSSIBLE BY ...: The Death of Public Broadcasting in the United States *by James Ledbetter*

IMAGINING HOME: Class, Culture and Nationalism in the African Diaspora *by Sidney Lemelle and Robin D. G. Kelley*

TWICE THE WORK OF FREE LABOR: The Political Economy of Convict Labor in the New South *by Alex Lichtenstein*

DANGEROUS CROSSROADS: Popular Music, Postmodernism and the Poetics of Place *by George Lipsitz*

BLACK AMERICAN POLITICS: From the Washington Marches to Jesse Jackson *by Manning Marable*

THE OTHER SIDE: Los Angeles from Both Sides of the Border *by Ruben Martinez*

AN INJURY TO ALL: The Decline of American Unionism *by Kim Moody*

WORKERS IN A LEAN WORLD: Unions in the International Economy *by Kim Moody*

YOUTH, IDENTITY, POWER: The Sixties Chicano Movement *by Carlos Muñoz Jr*

SELLING CULTURE: Magazines, Markets and Class at the Turn of the Century *by Richard Ohmann*

RED DIRT: Growing Up Okie *by Roxanne Dunbar Ortiz*

ANOTHER TALE TO TELL: Politics and Narrative in Postmodern Culture *by Fred Pfeil*

WHITE GUYS: Studies in Postmodern Domination and Difference *by Fred Pfeil*

THEY MUST BE REPRESENTED: The Politics of Documentary *by Paula Rabinowitz*

PROFESSORS, POLITICS AND POP *by Jon Wiener*

DEVELOPMENT ARRESTED: The Blues and Plantation Power in the Mississippi Delta *by Clyde Woods*

THE LEFT AND THE DEMOCRATS *The Year Left 1*

TOWARDS A RAINBOW SOCIALISM *The Year Left 2*

RESHAPING THE US LEFT: Popular Struggles in the 1980s *The Year Left 3*

FIRE IN THE HEARTH: The Radical Politics of Place in America *The Year Left 4*